Thomas Hardy's Novels

A Study Guide

Thomas Hardy's Novels

A Study Guide

by

MAUREEN MAHON

HEINEMANN EDUCATIONAL BOOKS

LONDON

Heinemann Educational Books Ltd
LONDON EDINBURGH MELBOURNE AUCKLAND TORONTO
HONG KONG SINGAPORE KUALA LUMPUR
IBADAN NAIROBI JOHANNESBURG
LUSAKA NEW DELHI KINGSTON

ISBN 0 435 18552 7

This little book is dedicated in memory of my mother, Mary G. Mahon (died 7-3-1967), to whose constant support I owe any critical abilities I possess, and who would have read this work with interest.

Published by
Heinemann Educational Books Ltd
48 Charles Street, London W1X 8AH
Printed in Great Britain by
Biddles of Guildford, Martyr Road,
Guildford, Surrey

Contents

Preface

This book is designed principally for students of Hardy's major novels at GCE 'A' Level, and in the early stages of university study. The greater part of the space is devoted to a detailed analysis of the six novels generally recognized as major, but brief reference is also made to Hardy's poems, and to the minor novels and short stories. In addition, an introductory chapter covers Hardy's life, and final chapters give a general survey of his position in his own era, his strengths and weaknesses, and his overall achievement.

At the level for which this book is designed, it is likely that only one or two texts will be set for detailed study. Clearly, the first aim of the student should be to know the prescribed texts thoroughly. But, for purposes of comparison, and for the answering of general questions on Hardy's art, it will be a distinct advantage to have read a further number of the novels, not necessarily in the same detail.

Restrictions of space make it impossible to quote from the novels as fully as one would wish, and specific passages have often been referred to rather than quoted. The student should always support his analysis by direct quotation where possible.

Thomas Hardy is a novelist who is somewhat out of favour with influential modern critics, possibly because many of them are urban dwellers who fail to appreciate Hardy's distinctive portrayal of country life. While his defects are not disguised in this book, I have tried to give full weight to the substantial gifts that make him still a widely read and widely respected writer. His integrity and total unworldliness shine through all his work, and his deep compassion for human suffering, and tenderness for the unfortunate denote a sensibility more than ever needed in an age when violence, brutality, and cynicism are all too prevalent.

Examinations, though important and essential, are not the prime aim of study, particularly in English literature, and it is hoped that this book will help the reader to understand and appreciate more fully the distinctive gifts of Hardy as a novelist of tragic vision, and an unrivalled delineator of English rural life.

I should like to express my thanks to all who have helped me in preparing this work, and in particular to the authorities of the British Library, the Southampton University Library, and the Portsmouth City Libraries, from all of whom I obtained valuable critical work on Hardy.

1
Thomas Hardy

Thomas Hardy was born in 1840 in the village of Higher
Bockhampton in Dorset, the son of a builder and mason. He lived
in a comparatively comfortable and congenial home, where
serious reading and music were encouraged; he learned to play the
violin early and, as a boy, often played for village dances and fes-
tivities. Hardy's experience of sharing in the rural communal life
when young was to give him a profound knowledge of the lives of
ordinary poor country people; and later, when he had moved a
safe distance from his origins, he was to depict lives such as these
with sympathy and humanity in his greatest novels.

Hardy received his secondary education, which included Greek
and Latin, at a day school in Dorchester. At sixteen, he left to be
apprenticed to a Dorchester architect, John Hicks. Hicks, himself
interested in intellectual questions, allowed his apprentices
considerable latitude; Hardy enjoyed many lively discussions at his
place of work, and also continued the habit of regular study learnt
at school, reading the classics, English and French literature, and
philosophical and theological works. During this time, Hardy met
Horace Moule, son of a clerical family and a distinguished
classical scholar, who became a lifelong friend. Moule had
considerable intellectual influence over Hardy, and in particular
introduced him to current journals and reviews which had the
effect of causing Hardy to question his earlier strong religious
beliefs. (See chapter 8 for further information.) As a boy, Hardy
had been devout, and the question of his attending a university
and becoming a clergyman may have been considered; but, if
Hardy had entertained any such ambitions, his increasing scepticism, which emerges very clearly in his novels, must have caused
him to abandon such plans. The failure of Moule's career and his
eventual suicide in 1873 were tragic blows to Hardy.

At this time, Hardy also got to know William Barnes, a poet

and schoolteacher who was living in Dorchester. The influence of Barnes, who wrote in local dialect, may have encouraged Hardy to use in both verse and prose the speech of ordinary people, although he was careful to avoid those extreme forms of dialect which made Barnes's work largely unintelligible to the average reader.

Life in London

In 1862, Hardy moved to work in an architect's office in London, where he remained for five years. The sophistication of the capital was a shock to the diffident but ambitious young man from the country. Hardy enjoyed all the normal pleasures of London life: the theatre, the opera, concerts, social engagements. In addition, he not only did well in architecture, in which he won a medal and a prize in competitions, but also found time to continue his general education, reading widely in the classics, in English literature, including contemporary poets and novelists, and in philosophy. In spite of these attainments, he remained somewhat lacking in self-assurance; he never felt, throughout his life, fully at ease in the modish flippancy of fashionable society, and he was always sensitive about his humble origins, which he felt obliged to conceal in the snobbish Victorian society of his day. Many of his novels show evidence of strong class feeling, the selfishness and triviality of the upper classes and the members of London society being unfavourably contrasted with the sincerity and altruism of ordinary people, especially the rural poor.

While he was in London Hardy began also the writing of poetry, a pursuit that he was to continue throughout his life. All his early poems were rejected by editors, and it was not until 1875 that he succeeded in publishing his first poem. His poetry was already promising, showing great originality and a distinctive feeling for the use of words.

It was also while he was in London that Hardy, who continued to read the most celebrated sceptical Victorian thinkers, finally abandoned the Church and orthodox belief. As was natural in a young man who had been pious in boyhood, the intellectual necessity, as he saw it, of repudiating religious beliefs profoundly saddened him. He was sensitive to the sufferings of humanity, both that of others and his own, and already conscious of the harshness of life, and his conviction that Man was not aided in his difficulties by any supernatural force made him deeply pessimistic. His belief was that human beings were the products of evolutionary and environmental forces over which they had virtually no control, being possessed of, at the most, only a limited degree of free will. In spite of people's efforts to do good, their happiness and achievement, or the lack of them, depended mainly on chance and 'senseless circumstance'. This bleak creed is exemplified many times in Hardy's novels in the sad destinies of many of his best-known characters: Tess and Jude, Michael Henchard, Eustacia Vye, Giles Winterborne.

Return to Dorset

Either because of working too hard in London, or as the result of too many pressures, Hardy's health began to suffer from what seems to have been mainly nervous debility. He returned to Dorset in 1867, where he continued his architectural work in his old master Hicks's office, and his health was soon restored in the less stressful routine of Dorchester. But the London illness indicates that, although basically a healthy man, he was not exceptionally robust; a lack of stamina may have contributed to his melancholy outlook on life.

The return home was marked by the development of a love affair. Hardy as a young man was frequently attracted to different girls, but in most cases his interest was short-lived. Now, however, he became seriously attached to his cousin, Tryphena Sparks, of Puddletown, near Bockhampton, and may have become engaged to her. The affair was later broken off, on grounds which are not known, and Tryphena subsequently became a schoolmistress. In 1870, Hardy met Emma Lavinia Gifford, a high-spirited young woman who attracted him by her vitality, her enthusiasm for poetry, and her sympathy for his writing ambitions. She was of a higher social level than Hardy, being the daughter of a solicitor and niece of a Canon and former college Fellow, and her consciousness of her higher social position was one of the many factors which later were to estrange the pair from each other. They were married in 1874.

First novels

In Dorset, Hardy found time to write a somewhat naive first novel,

The Poor Man and the Lady, which he submitted to Macmillan. The story depicts a young architect of humble origin (very obviously based on Hardy himself), who falls in love with a squire's daughter; the opposition of the girl's father to the affair brings about tragic results. Hardy was later to repeat frequently this theme of the poor young man in love with a girl of a higher social level. The novel is chiefly interesting as evidence of Hardy's strong class feeling at the time, every opportunity being taken to castigate upper-class life, and to compare fashionable London society unfavourably with country life — a reflection, no doubt, of Hardy's own disenchantment with the capital. Macmillan rejected the book mainly because of the excessively derogatory picture drawn of the upper classes, and of the absurdity of some of the episodes.

Hardy's next effort was written largely to the recipe given by George Meredith, then Chapman and Hall's reader, who, after reading *The Poor Man and the Lady,* suggested that he should try a quite different type of book, with a more complex plot. The result was *Desperate Remedies,* published in 1871 by Tinsley, a highly melodramatic novel modelled on the works of Wilkie Collins. The story, which centres round the steward of an estate's manslaughter of his first wife, with the aim of leaving him free to marry the heroine, is frequently far-fetched in its complicated intrigues, but there are many passages in which Hardy's narrative or descriptive skills show unmistakeable promise as a novelist. Reviewers did not miss the novel's weaknesses; much of the melodrama was sharply criticized. The book as a result did not sell well, and Hardy lost money on it. At the same time, many reviewers gave high praise to the author's vivid descriptions of the Dorset coast or of scenes of village life. It was typical of Hardy, and was to remain a weakness during his career as a novelist, that he was reduced to near despair by the hostile criticisms, and was little cheered by the more favourable comments.

Hardy's second accepted novel, *Under the Greenwood Tree,* published in 1872, was a more significant venture. In this slight, graceful work, which has been over-praised in the past, the young writer wisely restricted himself to the milieu which he knew from first hand: the rural life of the Wessex peasantry. The plot is of the simplest, and the book's chief claims to distinction lie in the unforced comedy of the scenes of rural life, and the pithy, humorous dialogue of the rustic characters. It is the most light-hearted of all Hardy's novels, for he is here showing the country people mainly in their moments of relaxation, the story being concerned chiefly with the doings of the choir and orchestra of the little village of Mellstock, who are ousted from their traditional role as providers of church music by an organ introduced by the new vicar. The economic problems of the country village and the everyday reality of hard toil for meagre rewards are largely ignored by Hardy in this novel, in which he is in virtually a holiday mood. He skilfully introduces a related sub-plot, built around Fancy Day, a new village schoolmistress, who also becomes the new organist, and who is courted by three men in the village, including the Vicar. Fancy's eventual acceptance of Dick Dewy, a young tranter who sings in the choir, possibly symbolizes the ability of the old traditional order to assimilate the newcomer. But it would be a mistake to stress unduly the more serious issues which emerge from the novel; Hardy has merely indicated these without developing them. The book, although essentially minor, is important because it indicates the field in which Hardy's real talent lay, and shows that, if he were to develop more serious themes, he had the capacity to become a major writer.

Hardy was encouraged by the comparative success of *Under the Greenwood Tree* to attempt a more ambitious work. *A Pair of Blue Eyes,* published in 1873, is a novel of greater scope, concerning a diffident, immature young heroine, Elfride, who is tormented by mainly groundless feelings of guilt about an innocent first romance, and, through a lack of moral courage, lies about this youthful attachment to her second and more mature suitor, Knight. The latter is an exacting and jealous man who cannot endure the idea of any prior attachment in the life of the girl he loves; he breaks off the engagement with Elfride when he hears of the earlier romance, in the mistaken belief that she has been the mistress of her first admirer, and a tragic ending results. The book marks an advance in character portrayal, and also contains many excellent descriptions of the Cornish landscape, but, on the whole, Hardy was probably unwise to abandon the rural scene and its characters for an environment of which he had a more limited understanding. *A Pair of Blue Eyes* was the first novel of Hardy's to be serialized prior to its publication in book form; all his subsequent fiction was also serialized first. (In this guide, the dates of publication given are, except where otherwise stated, the dates of appearance in book form.)

The mature novels

In 1874 Hardy published what is generally considered his first major work. *Far From the Madding Crowd* (see Chapter 2 for detailed analysis). A number of characteristics distinguish this novel as major. The themes with which it deals are serious and important ones, which matter to the reader. The characters are not mere stock types or half-developed sketches, but full portraits of complex individuals whose strengths, weaknesses, and needs are understood and vividly depicted by their creator. Action arises convincingly from the characters' dispositions. There is a new and distinctive grasp of the relation of the characters to their rural environment, which is both their source of livelihood and a main influence in forming their personalities. Also, for the first time, Hardy in this novel succeeds in integrating his language with his ideas; through the use of poetic imagery, he links the actions or the states of mind of the characters with other phenomena in nature, thereby showing the poet's grasp of the essential unity of all creation.

With the publication of *Far From the Madding Crowd,* Hardy established his position as a novelist of serious calibre. From 1874 until he concluded his novel-writing career with the publication of *The Well-Beloved* in 1897, he wrote ten more novels. Five of these, in addition to *Far From the Madding Crowd,* may be ranked as major works, *The Return of the Native* (1878), *The Mayor of Casterbridge* (1886), *The Woodlanders* (1887), *Tess of the d'Urbervilles* (1891), and *Jude the Obscure* (1895). The publication of these was interspersed with minor works, so that Hardy cannot be regarded as a writer who shows a consistent path of development.

If we consider solely the major works, what is chiefly remarkable in them is the increasingly sombre nature of Hardy's vision. *Far From the Madding Crowd* is a comparatively optimistic book, with a relatively happy ending rewarding the hero and heroine; in it, the rural environment is depicted as challenging and dangerous, but as being capable of being mastered by man's hard work and intelligent awareness so that it serves his needs. But in later novels, Hardy portrays his characters increasingly as the victims of a fate that is mainly malevolent, tragically powerless to avert catastrophe by their efforts to do good. The environment is now depicted as mainly indifferent to man, but also even positively inimical (especially in *The Return of the Native* and *The Woodlanders*), reducing characters to loneliness and poverty and eventually destroying them. Hardy also shows an increasing tendency to attribute his characters' unhappy destinies partly to outmoded social institutions and conventions. In *The Woodlanders* and *Jude the Obscure* he criticizes the over-rigid marriage laws that refuse to allow divorce in cases of incompatibility; in *Tess* he attacks the Victorian convention that a woman who loses her virginity has necessarily a bad moral character; and in *Jude* he questions the class structure of society that bars the way to education for able working-class people. Many reviewers and members of the reading public were outraged by the attacks on conventional concepts of morality expressed in *Tess* and *Jude,* and the amount of carping criticism which these works received was the main reason why the too-sensitive Hardy gave up novel-writing altogether.

Hardy as poet

Hardy continued to compose poems during the years of novel-writing, and, as he became increasingly disillusioned by the reception given to his fiction, his poems became more important to him. In 1898, he published *Wessex Poems and other Verses,* a miscellaneous collection of poems, most of which had been written long before; he published eight collections of poems in all.

His poems, most of which are quite short, have for their subjects reflections on life and on the scheme of things, moments of significance recalled in memory, brief tales in verse, and the recounting of simple incidents in the lives of ordinary people. Well-known short pieces include 'In Time of the Breaking of Nations', a poem which stresses how ordinary life continues unchanged in spite of great historical events; 'When I Set out for

Lyonnese', a brief lyric of memory; 'A Broken Appointment', a brief relection on a single incident; and 'The Ruined Maid', an example of Hardy's humour in verse.

From what has been said of the subjects of the majority of Hardy's poems, it can be seen that there is a parallel between these and the themes of his major novels. In many of the poems the philosophy expressed in the novels can also be discerned: a sense of the contrast between the concerns and puny efforts of man and the vast impersonal indifference of the universe, and a consciousness of the fatality that often thwarts human plans; 'The Convergence of the Twain' (lines on the loss of the *Titanic*) expresses well Hardy's sense of the mysterious fate that overshadows all human endeavours.

Hardy's poems are often distinguished by unusual language, and by the skilful use of irregular rhythm, although, like his novels, they are sometimes marred by awkward expressions and clumsy circumlocutions. His status among poets today is high, and many modern critics rate him, as a poet, above his standing as a novelist.

Hardy's most ambitious poem was *The Dynasts*, an epic drama in three parts (the first part published 1903), treating of the Napoleonic Wars. This lengthy poem allows Hardy to express his views about casualty and fate more fully than anywhere else in his writing.

Hardy as short story writer

Hardy also published four volumes of short stories, many of which were written long before their publication in collected form. These were *Wessex Tales* (1888), *A Group of Noble Dames* (1891), *Life's Little Ironies* (1894), and *A Changed Man; The Waiting Supper and Other Tales* (1913). These stories are of very uneven quality. The best of them contain neat twists of plot and touches of irony, and a few, such as *The Fiddler of the Reels* and *Barbara of the House of Grebe* are memorable because of the author's skill in creating atmosphere. In the plots of his tales, Hardy draws freely upon oral tradition, especially in his frequent use of the supernatural. Yet, in spite of the high quality of some of the stories *(The Withered Arm, A Son's Veto, A Mere Interlude)*, Hardy does not impress as a natural short story writer. His style lacks the economy and tautness needed for success in this genre, and the circumlocutions and digressions that can easily be accepted in a long novel are serious flaws in the short form. Some of the tales read more like short novels in miniature than true short stories.

The latter years and second marriage

The course of Hardy's own life was not in itself tragic, but often chequered and unsatisfactory. His marriage went well for a short time, the couple living first in Surbiton, then at Sturminster in Dorset, where they spent their happiest days together. After another period in London, they moved back again to Dorset. In 1885, they settled in Max Gate, Dorchester, a house built to Hardy's specifications, and Hardy remained there, though always with frequent visits elsewhere, until his death in 1928. The later years of the marriage were made unhappy by wide divergences of opinion between Hardy and his wife. Mrs Hardy, who always retained a sense of social superiority to her husband, wanted more social life than he was willing to engage in, and was made increasingly unhappy by his agnosticism, the attacks on conventional morality, and on marriage contained in his later novels, and by the publication of poems revealing his earlier attachments to other women. Although Emma Hardy had earlier encouraged her husband to write, his eventual success appears to have caused her more jealousy than pride, and she even imagined that her own amateur literary efforts were superior to Hardy's own work. In spite of these causes of hostility, Hardy seems to have retained an affection for Emma, based on their early days of courtship and marriage, and was deeply distressed at her death in 1912. Hardy's second wife, Florence Dugdale, whom he married in 1914, seems to have been proud of his now established literary fame, and careful to secure comfort and tranquillity; nevertheless, this marriage does not seem to have been outstandingly happy either. It is possible that Hardy, like many very gifted men, was difficult to live with. He received the Order of Merit in 1910, and, after his death in 1928, his ashes were interred in Westminster Abbey.

What chiefly interests the critic in surveying Hardy's life is the reason for his sombre outlook. He seems to have begun life with normal youthful optimism, but the gloom set in early, so that by the time he came to write the majority of his important works, his vision was one which stressed, possibly to an excessive degree, the sadness and the difficulties of life. Probably his loss of religious belief was the most important single cause of his melancholy, conditioning as it did Hardy's whole concept of Man's life and future destiny; to believe that a human being was primarily the product of evolution and environment, and subject to the vagaries of chance, was not a creed likely to imbue a thoughtful author with very hopeful ideas of what his characters could achieve through their own efforts.

Many of the circumstances of Hardy's life also contributed to his sadness: his humble background, a factor inducing discomfort in the snobbish society of Victorian England; personal tragedies such as the death of his friend Moule and his unsatisfactory marriage; the lukewarm reception given to his books by at least some critics, and the charges of immorality brought against works written with deep seriousness and integrity. Yet possibly the deepest causes of Hardy's melancholy lay in his own disposition. Like many artists, he was shy, acutely sensitive, diffident, secretive; such a nature ensured that he was more acutely wounded by the sorrows and disappointments of life than a coarser individual would have been.

In the main, Hardy's was a sad life, in which his gifts received recognition very late, and it is correct to describe his outlook as pessimistic. From his sad outlook, however, he created memorable novels which, pointing as they do to the universal prevalence of sadness and suffering, indicate a truth which no improvement in material or social conditions can alter. He is a great novelist because he is a born story-teller, who expresses his vision of the world through narratives that hold the reader's interest, and who expresses his view of Man's predicament through the actions and feelings of characters who are vividly and triumphantly alive. He is also England's foremost regional novelist, who describes the life of the Wessex countryside with a fidelity and accuracy that have no equal, and he does so in prose which, at its best, has the poet's gift of showing by the skilful use of language the unity of Man with his natural environment.

2

Far From the Madding Crowd

At the end of 1872 Hardy arranged with Leslie Stephen, editor of the *Cornhill Magazine* and a distinguished man of letters, who had admired *Under the Greenwood Tree,* to produce as a serial for his magazine, a pastoral tale whose chief characters would probably be a woman-farmer, a shepherd, and a sergeant of cavalry. The result was *Far From the Madding Crowd,* serialized in the *Cornhill* during 1874, and published in book form at the end of that year. To work under the scrutiny of such a gifted editor was a useful experience for Hardy, and Stephen suggested to him a number of omissions and amendments that improved the novel.

From the original rough concept of the book, which was of an old pastoral folk tale, with elements of the ballad, Hardy eventually produced what was to be the first of his major novels, the first work distinctively marked by his unique vision of life. He had matured greatly during 1872 and 1873, possibly because of his attachment to Emma Gifford, and the death by suicide of his friend Moule in 1873 had deepened his sense of the sadness of life. The new novel was to bear the marks of his greater maturity and gravity. The tale of the young woman-farmer, Bathsheba Everdene, who is loved both by the devoted shepherd, Gabriel Oak, and by the dashing but faithless sergeant Troy, develops far beyond the limits of the stock model on which it is based, the characters and their complex and shifting relationships being depicted with psychological insight and mature irony. The ballad element survives only to a slight degree, for instance in the singing of Bathsheba and the flute-playing of Gabriel Oak, and the simplicity of characterization typical of a ballad form is left far behind. Hardy eventually increased the gravity of the work by adding to the original three characters a fourth, the outwardly stolid but inwardly inflammable farmer Boldwood, whose immoderate passion for Bathsheba leads to disaster for both himself and Troy.

What finally emerged is a work of genuine achievement, representing a view of life which can be considered significant; a novel that shows up the essentially minor quality of *Under the Greenwood Tree* or the triviality of *A Pair of Blue Eyes*. The reader finds *Far From the Madding Crowd* important because what happens to the people in it seems to matter. For the first time, too, Hardy relates the lives of human and complex characters to their natural environment, which is not, as in *A Pair of Blue Eyes*, merely a subject for occasional patches of perceptive description, but the order and background to which all the characters are constantly related. There exists throughout this novel a harmonious relation between the narration of events or states of mind and the natural order. Because of these achievements, the book can fairly be considered to be Hardy's first major work.

Themes

The main theme of the book is the disparity between romance and reality. The four main characters are all shown as being initially in the grip of false romantic illusions; their loves, which are really infatuations, are based on idealization rather than on any realistic understanding of the objects of their affections. Bathsheba's infatuation for Troy is based on a mere surface impression of him as a dashing soldier of noble ancestry, a concept which Troy himself strengthens deliberately by acts such as his exhibition of sword play (Chapter XXVIII), and the gift of his watch to Bathsheba (Chapter XXVI). The sergeant also is in the grip of an illusion, suffering from a shallow infatuation with Bathsheba as an attractive woman and the owner of a desirable property; because of this, he deceives Bathsheba, and also ill-treats Fanny Robin, the woman whom he really loves. Farmer Boldwood's passion for Bathsheba rests on no more solid basis than her thoughtless prank of sending him a valentine, and he never gets near enough mentally to her to understand that any concessions she makes to him result, not from love, but from pity and a sense of blameworthiness. His absurd love makes him dangerously oblivious of reality; it leads him to an almost total withdrawal from the everyday world into a private realm of obsession, as is shown by his unbalanced behaviour in storing up in his home jewels and clothes for Bathsheba in the hope that she will become his wife years later (Chapter LV). Even the love of Oak, who is by far the most steady and mature of the characters, is initially based on a romantic idealization of Bathsheba. He knows nothing about her nature; he merely sees a pretty girl admiring herself in a mirror, or riding her horse with high-spirited tomboyishness, and is unwise enough to propose to marry her on these slender foundations. So, all four main characters are in love largely with the products of their own imaginations.

Allied to this first theme of romance versus reality is the concept of regeneration through suffering, a theme found often in Hardy The main characters who survive (Bathsheba and Gabriel Oak) learn through suffering to reject false versions of romance and base their happiness on the reality of tried affection. When Oak finally secures marriage to Bathsheba, his love for her has a different quality. He has been near to Bathsheba, in the position of a hired hand, for a considerable time—long enough to watch her mistakes in dealing with Troy, and to be the recipient of her confidences about both Troy and Boldwood; by now he understands her and accepts her weaknesses. Bathsheba herself, whose character in the early part of the book is flawed by the pride and self-sufficiency induced by prosperity and independence, learns through misfortune to appreciate Oak's steady devotion to her interests, and the honesty that underlines his frequent plain speaking. When these two characters marry, their union is based on a mature appreciation of each other's faults and virtues.

Bathsheba and Gabriel Oak achieve a measure of happiness because they are willing to learn from their errors. Troy and Boldwood, neither of whom is prepared to amend those characteristics or attitudes that lead to unhappiness, are both destroyed, each becoming, ironically, the agent of the other's ruin. The novel shows a preoccupation with the concept of a social order, to which characters must learn to conform. Those individuals who submit to the social discipline eventually prosper; those who do not meet destruction. Troy and Boldwood cannot, because of their different kinds of egoism, live within the ordinary social code, and, as a result, the fate of the first is a violent death, and of the second ruin and life imprisonment.

The second, and almost equally important, theme of the book is the relation of the human characters to their natural environment, and, in particular, the problem of wresting a livelihood from natural resources. Nature, as always in Hardy, can show herself dangerous and malignant, as Oak soon finds when his carelessness in keeping a wild young sheepdog and in failing to fence off a steep cliff results in the destruction of his flock and, with it, the loss of his status of independent farmer. In this novel, however, unlike others, Hardy depicts nature as more truly a 'neutral' than an inimical force. Certainly, she sends deadly trials, notably the great storm that threatens Bathsheba's unprotected stacks of corn on the night of the harvest-supper; yet, at the same time, she gives ample warning, to those who understand her, of the approaching bad weather through the observable behaviour of animals and insects (Chapter XXXVI). Nature is always potentially threatening, but the natural environment can be conquered and made to serve man's needs by skill, hard work, and vigilance.

The ability to master the natural environment is exemplified in the novel by Gabriel Oak, a man who understands the natural world in which he lives. Oak saves Bathsheba's fortunes on three occasions: he extinguishes a fire which threatens to destroy her ricks; he cures her sheep when they are in convulsions; and he covers the stacks of grain in time to protect them from the great storm. He averts disaster by promptness, hard and dedicated work, and, above all, because of specialized knowledge; Oak is the man who, in emergencies, knows what to do. And, to an extent unusual in Hardy, Gabriel's patient, intelligent efforts, made initially in adversity, are rewarded by success and prosperity. His success story is an answer to those who maintain that Hardy's novels always represent unrelieved sadness. For once, it seems, fate can be kind to man's efforts, and Gabriel's eventual happiness and prosperity make this the most optimistic and, in some ways, the best-balanced of all Hardy's great novels.

These two main themes, that of reality versus romance, and of the problem of mastering the environment, are linked to each other because Hardy depicts genuine realistic love as connected with the primary task of earning a living. The idealizing infatuations of the characters have no connection with the everyday world of work. The marriage between Troy and Bathsheba can never be a sound economic partnership, any more than it can be a genuine union of hearts, for Troy lacks both the skills and the personal qualities needed to manage a farm as conspicuously as he is lacking in the attributes of fidelity and kindness which make affection lasting. The love affair of these two exists in an unreal world of pretty words, idle compliments, and the surface brilliance of a display of swordsmanship. Similarly, Boldwood's passion for Bathsheba is expressed in solitary broodings, and in a romantic idealization which makes him shrink from the idea of doing normal farming business with her. By contrast, the affection of Bathsheba and Oak is based solidly on numerous experiences of shared work and mutual help. The resultant mutual cameraderie is, Hardy asserts, the best form of love.

> . . . the compounded feeling proves itself to be the only love which is strong as death — that love which many waters cannot quench, nor the floods drown, beside which the passion usually called by the name is evanescent as steam.

The biblical allusion in this quotation should be noted.

It is to be remarked that those of the characters who fail in personal relationships fail also in the economic test. Troy is not only faithless and selfish in his marital life; economically he is a parasite, contributing nothing to the farm by either management or manual work. Boldwood, initially a good farmer, neglects his crops and leaves his corn uncovered when he is depressed by unsuccessful love, and so courts material disaster.

Plot and narrative

One is struck by the sheer narrative energy of this novel, which expresses itself in a succession of memorable events; the plot is constantly developing, and numerous striking incidents linger in the mind (serial requirements of course account to some degree for the multiplicity of striking incidents). Most of these incidents, even those which on the face of it seem somewhat theatrical, carry conviction because they show actions which are in keeping with what we have previously learnt of the characters. For example, the central scene of the book, that in which Bathsheba opens Fanny's coffin, risks being theatrical, but in fact carries conviction because Bathsheba's state of jealous anxiety has been so gradually and artistically built up that her dramatic action seems to represent the obvious and only means by which she can resolve her doubts about her husband. Boldwood's shooting of Troy risks being melodramatic, but succeeds because the immoderate passion of the farmer has been so convincingly depicted that this act of violence seems an inevitable result.

Of course, as often in Hardy, some incidents do seem somewhat far-fetched or coincidental. It is rather an unlikely coincidence, although one possibly justified by the needs of the plot, that Oak should save from fire the ricks that happen to belong to Bathsheba, and that she, at exactly the same time, should happen to need a shepherd. Fanny's mixing-up the churches for her intended wedding, though possible, is somewhat unconvincing, given her anxiety to secure marriage to Troy. Bathsheba's failure to recognize Fanny when the distressed girl accosts her husband on the way home from the races is unaccountable, and perhaps merely a careless slip on Hardy's part. The weakest section in the whole book is that which describes Troy's escape from drowning, travels in America, and reappearance near home in the role of performer in a travelling circus; this is all pretty incredible, and shows a flagging in creative vitality and a resultant recourse to unconvincing invention. But the novel recovers with the return of Troy to Weatherbury to claim his wife, and is built up to a tragic and memorable climax.

Note how Hardy sometimes gains in effect by using an indirect method, rather than actual description, to convey action. The coffin scene gains by the author's subtlety in not actually describing the moment when Bathsheba opens the coffin. The shock of the revelation is indirectly, and tellingly, conveyed by Bathsheba's succeeding husky, broken-hearted words: "It was best to know the worst, and I know it now!" Similarly, the narrative gains from the fact that Fanny's death in childbirth in the Union is not described, but merely reported; this allows Hardy to show more convincingly the gradual build-up of rumour in the neighbourhood concerning the girl's death, and to create a measure of suspense about the circumstances of her end.

In this novel, Hardy has apparently not allowed himself to be worried by the problem of the 'point of view' of the narrative. He solves this quite simply by causing the action to be seen through the eyes of all the chief characters in turn.

It is no accident that this novel has been made into a good film, because it is distinguished by a series of impressively vivid pictures. The pastoral world is a perpetually shifting landscape, and Hardy depicts its shifts and contrasts with an acute eye for telling detail. The description of the great storm (Chapter XXXVII) is a marvel of descriptive prose, every single flash of lightning being distinguished from the others in some way by the narrator. The many other descriptions of the natural world are made memorable by the author's sheer knowledge, based on acute observation; even the least countrified of readers grasps the fact that Hardy genuinely *knows* the world of sheep and sheep-shearing, of crops and animals and insects. Nor does detailed observation preclude a wider vision; there are many impressive pictures of the sky and the stars, which suggest the immensity of the universe outside the small unit of Weatherbury.

To the descriptions of nature, Hardy adds memorable vivid pictures of the characters: Bathsheba admiring herself in the mirror; the burning ricks and Oak's grimy, smudged appearance; the shearers sitting at the shearing supper with their heads and shoulders bathed in light; the central dramatic scenes of the coffin-opening and the killing of Troy. A considerable part of Hardy's art is to link the appearance of the landscape to mental states. The picture of Fanny outside the barracks conveys brilliantly the sense of the young woman's isolation; Troy is made physically inaccessible to her by the barriers of the river and the barrack walls, in a manner that parallels the mental inaccessibility induced by his carelessness and by his temporary preoccupation with some other girl whom he has picked up. Again, the picture of Troy, newly married, framed in the farmhouse window, expresses well his triumph at his successful marriage, and conjures up a mood which contrasts strongly with the dejected state of the rejected Oak. Boldwood is frequently presented against dawns and sunsets of unpredictable weather, in a way that suggests the equally unpredictable nature of the potentially violent farmer's behaviour.

Hardy sometimes heightens this unity of the physical world and the mental states of the characters by the poetic use of images which, if sometimes rather obvious, are still effective. The courtship of Bathsheba by Troy commences with the heroine having her dress accidentally caught in the sergeant's spur, and is furthered by Troy's display of sword play in the ferns. These images convey simply the manner in which Bathsheba is won over by the martial power of the dashing soldier, and the extent to which she falls a victim to surface glamour. The dance of death which the great storm seems to enact possibly symbolizes both the death of love and trust that Bathsheba already feels, and the future violent death of Troy which will darken her life; while the swamp beside which she sleeps when she runs out of the farmhouse after her quarrel with Troy epitomizes the state of poisoned inertia to which her own emotional life has now declined.

The natural environment which Hardy describes is a pagan and non-religious environment. The world of the characters depends on the seasons, the crops, and the produce of flocks and herds; birth, mating, and death are the chief events in their obscure lives. Hardy, in describing the great barn, specifically asserts that the world of natural needs and essential work precedes and outlasts religious institutions; his description of the building is, in fact, a defiant proclamation of agnostic humanism. Yet in other ways the temper of this novel is almost Christian; in, for example, its emphasis on patient, uncomplaining efforts to do good. Oak's genuine goodness is depicted as nourished by quiet Bible reading and humble prayer, just as Troy's selfishness is linked to his neglect of all church-going. Bathsheba's life is viewed almost as a religious pilgrimage, in which she learns to abjure pride and self-will, and to value the sterling human qualities; the dawning of light in her mind near the end of the story is very simply illustrated by the mood in which she listens to the as yet innocent children singing, unaware, Newman's hymn, "Lead, kindly light".

The characters

Many critics have commented, quite justly, that Bathsheba, the central character, escapes very lightly the possible results of her follies, securing in the end a happiness that she does little to deserve. (Admittedly it is a very chastened and sober happiness, but that is the most that Hardy ever allows the main characters of his major novels.) In spite of the occasional fulminations against woman, which the author allows to intrude into the text, Bathsheba is dealt with almost lovingly, and often romanticized; she is viewed almost entirely from the outside, and her attractive, vital presence dominates the book. She wins the reader's sympathy both because her errors are human, and because they do not result from any malevolence. Hardy does not spare her weaknesses, depicting them indeed with great psychological insight. She is an adept at deceiving herself; she pretends to be angry at Troy's subtle flattery, which is cleverly expressed by reproaches at her disturbing charms, but is secretly deeply flattered by them; she goes to Bath pretending to herself that she intends to break with Troy, but is in fact still infatuated with him, so much so that she ends by marrying him there. Although she has earlier rejected Oak, it is noticeable that he is the one person whose opinion of herself she really cares about; and, in a very feminime way, she is piqued when he appears to withdraw any claims to her.

Oak and Troy are saved from being stock figures by shrewd touches of insight. Oak hovers on the edge of being an uninteresting epitome of devotion and unselfishness, but is redeemed from an impossible saintliness by a sturdy readiness to stand up to Bathsheba and to carry out some uncompromising plain speaking to her. Similarly, a certain psychological subtlety brings to life what might otherwise be the somewhat conventional figure of Sergeant Troy, outwardly gallant but inwardly corrupt. For instance, he is shown as being basically a philanderer, yet paradoxically more in earnest than he suspects when he courts Bathsheba. That he instinctively knows how to win over a capable woman is shown by his willingness, during the courtship, to help in the work of the farm — a pretence of interest that he immediately drops as soon as his aim of marriage is secured. His worst fault is perhaps his sentimentality. He selfishly neglects Fanny Robin when she is alive — it is clear that it is more his vanity than his love that is wounded by her non-appearance at the projected wedding — yet exerts himself to plant flowers on her grave when she is dead. (Even here, he is faint-hearted; the destruction of his work by water flowing from a gargoyle causes him to give up this too-tardy attempt at atonement.) Hardy has shown considerable skill in making his attractiveness to women believable. Troy is depicted as possessing a certain presence and dignity of manner; these attributes enable him to carry out successfully the sword-play scene, which, with another man, might have become merely ridiculous, and conspicuously give him the upper hand in the scene in which the desperate Boldwood tries to bribe him (Chapter XXXIV).

Boldwood himself is little more than a study of a single obsession, made interesting by its very excess; the disasters to which his unregulated emotions bring him serve as an answer to those who mistakenly think that Hardy approves of abandonment to passion. Fanny is predominantly the stock figure of the betrayed maiden, memorable only for her gentleness and her unwillingness to utter any reproaches to Troy. Her nightmare journey to the workhouse and her miserable death there are an implied indictment of a heartless society that does nothing to aid her in her distress; her only living support on that last journey is a humble dog, which, ironically, is stoned away by the Union officials.

This novel, like almost all Hardy's works, is often marred by bad style, exemplified by weightiness, awkward circumlocutions, cumbersome phrases and pretentious words. Consider, for example, the description of the great barn which has already been referred to; here, phrases such as 'this abraded pile' and 'a satisfied sense of functional continuity' sound awkward and ponderous. Chapter VIII, which describes the scene in Warren's malthouse, contains some noticeable example of Hardy's stylistic failures: the description of the room itself, for instance; or the very bad paragraph, commenting on one of the rustics' speeches, which commences, 'A meditation on the obvious inference . . .'.

However, in justice to Hardy, two facts must also be noted: first, that passages of cumbersome writing are often partly redeemed by precisely observed descriptive detail; and secondly, that the sweep and energy of the narrative of this novel tend to carry the reader easily across the worst passages. Some paragraphs, such as that on the great barn, can be criticized both for awkward writing and for the author's overt intrusion into the text; but the passage nevertheless arouses interest in the philosophy expressed in it. Hardy quite simply often succeeds in spite of stylistically faulty narrative or comment because he has something important to say.

Much the same comment can be made on the dialogue. It is sometimes weighty, stilted, and unnatural, as in the following speech of Boldwood to Bathsheba (Chapter XXXI):

'Your dear love, Bathsheba, is such a vast thing beside your pity, that the loss of your pity as well as your love is no great addition to my sorrow, nor does the gain of your pity make it sensibly less. O sweet — how dearly you spoke to me behind the spear-bed at the washing-pool, and in the barn at the shearing, and that dearest last time in the evening at your home!'

There is much poetry in the second half of this extract, but, in the main, it is an example of bad dialogue; it is both stiff and wordy. Yet, once again, the whole of this chapter, in which Boldwood bitterly blames Bathsheba for preferring Troy to himself, is better than many of its parts. In spite of wordy patches, the *cumulative* effect of the chapter is to convey effectively the powerful emotions felt by the farmer. In any case, one must not judge Hardy chiefly by his lapses; he sometimes writes excellent simple dialogue, as in the starkly moving exchanges between Troy and Bathsheba in the scene following the coffin-opening, or in some of the quarrels between Bathsheba and Gabriel.

The 'rustic chorus' of the ordinary country folk deserves a brief comment. As often in Hardy, the rustics' role in the book is chiefly that of giving light relief to a serious story, and the salty humour of the conversation in Warren's malthouse or at the paying of the farmhands' wages is genuinely entertaining. Some critics have described the ordinary country people in this novel as corrupt, and in need of revitalization by the newcomers (Oak and Bathsheba), but that perhaps is an over-serious view. Certainly, the limitations of the farm workers, understandable because of limited opportunities, are not disguised. Oak's resourcefulness underlines their frequent helplessness, and the general lack of much sense of responsibility is illustrated by Joseph Poorglass's careless treatment of Fanny's coffin. The rustics have restricted minds, and their conversation consists mainly of homespun philosophy, discussions of personal idiosyncracies, and ordinary plain gossip. Yet they also show real virtues: kindliness and good neighbourliness, loyalty to their mistress, and a willingness to respond when shown (usually by Oak) what to do. It is true that they are led into drunkenness, to the neglect of duty, by Troy at the harvest supper, but it is the ex-sergeant, who threatens the farm people with dismissal if they do not join in the orgy, who is chiefly to blame. Here, a weak economic position makes the rustics malleable.

Far From the Madding Crowd may be summed up as a novel which, while lacking the greatness of vision of Hardy's best work, is an impressive book dealing both seriously and sensitively with major issues of life and love, wrong choices and later repentance, and with the relationship of man to the natural environment on which his livelihood depends.

3

The Return of the Native

Far From the Madding Crowd was a very successful novel,
securing for its author laudatory reviews and substantial earnings,
and establishing him as a writer of great promise. Hardy followed
this success by publishing, early in 1876, a new novel, *The Hand
of Ethelberta,* featuring a heroine who tries to establish herself in
smart society by exploiting her literary gifts and concealing her
humble origins (a situation which has obvious parallels with
Hardy's own life). The book, which is an attempt at both social
comedy and social satire, is not impressive, and was a disappointment to the critics. The tone fluctuates uneasily between comedy,
satire, and farce; the situations are often unconvincing and the
satire frequently lacks bite. Hardy reveals in this novel his perpetual inability to portray fashionable London life with any
conviction; few people are less good than he at describing a society
dinner party.

In contrast to this trivial minor work, Hardy's next novel, *The
Return of the Native* (1878), in which he wisely returns to the
rural life which he understands, is a work of memorable tragic
grandeur. It is marked by a deepening of his pessimism, and the
emergence of a stark tragic vision that is unameliorated by the
relative cheerfulness of *Far From the Madding Crowd*. In it, two
aspects which are distinctively characteristic of Hardy's best work
emerge for the first time: first, a preoccupation with fatality, and
a view of events in the universe as being determined by a chance
that is usually malevolent; secondly, a representation of nature
and the cosmos as indifferent and impersonal, and as caring
nothing for man's puny efforts to secure happiness or success.

Hardy's own life suggests some reasons for his deepening
pessimism. Marriage and literary success had together resulted in
his being absorbed by a cultivated class worlds removed from his
own humble background, and this uprooting seems to have

caused him considerable unhappiness. Again, though the early years of his marriage were the happiest, it may be that the disillusion with his wife and with their relationship which was to become so profound later was already beginning to appear. Finally, the unenthusiastic reviews of *The Hand of Ethelberta* further depressed the sensitive Hardy.

Themes

This book is primarily a novel of environment, because the milieu in which the characters live, stark, lonely Egdon Heath, conditions their lives more than any other factor. The whole of the first chapter is given to the description of the heath, an indication of its importance to the story. The impression that emerges from this chapter is of a place of gloom and solitude, which also is prehistoric and unalterable. For the first time, therefore, Hardy is presenting an environment which is not capable of being used and civilized by man. The heath is indifferent to, or could even be regarded as inimical to, the characters' attempts at doing good.

In such an unfriendly environment, Hardy cannot invoke the theme of the social discipline of shared work, which he so effectively used in *Far From the Madding Crowd*. No prospering enterprises are possible on Egdon—indeed, it is not clear how the ordinary cottagers earn a livelihood—and the main characters, who are almost all virtually unoccupied, are not united by any communal effort or shared mode of life. Equally, they are not linked by any shared leisure pursuits. The distances between their dwellings rule out the kind of mutual entertaining common in more compact rural communities; and, since the long journeys required and the risk of bad weather also discourage regular church-going, the predominantly middle-class chief characters have nowhere to meet each other. Eustacia, when she wants to meet the returned native, Clym Yeobright, has to resort to the stratagem, thought undignified in Victorian days, of dressing up in male clothing as one of the boys' mumming party.

In this lonely world, the main characters live in virtual isolation effectively subject to no social disciplines. This life, which possibly preserves these characters from the shoddier values of a more sophisticated society, seems to encourage at least some of them to reflect self-consciously about the purpose of their lives, but unfortunately also seems to nourish plans which will not stand the test of reality. Clym, who asks his mother, "What is well doing?", sincerely aspires both to genuine thought and to a life spent helping his fellow-men as a teacher, but he fails in both his aims; he is unequipped for the intellectual life towards which he strives, and he can offer his fellows only a self-acquired rag-bag philosophy which they show no sign of wanting. ' 'Tis good-hearted of the young man,' says one of the heath-dwellers whom Clym wishes to benefit. 'But, for my part, I think he had better mind his business.' Eustacia, even more foolishly, aspires to greatness, and vaguely yearns for a life of grandeur and luxury. She has no concept of the self-discipline required for the attainment of the first quality, nor of the unlikelihood that even sustained hard work (which she would never think of undertaking) will secure her the life of luxury she craves for. Wildeve, amorous and changeable, is probably merely seeking for happiness, without ever examining seriously whether his actions are likely to further his aim. The efforts of all these characters to secure fulfilment are feeble, and their puny attempts seem all the more insignificant when viewed against the background of the immutable, uncaring heath. The wishes and strivings of human beings count for little in this indifferent environment.

At a simpler level, the wild lonely heath exercises its influence on the dispositions of the characters, and therefore on their relations with each other. It makes Clym reflective, conscious of the needs of his fellows, and in tune with his environment; whereas its effect on Eustacia is to make her discontented and rebellious. The opposing reactions of these two to their life on the heath are largely responsible for their quarrel and the break-up of their marriage. Isolation on the heath also has the effect of making Wildeve restless and changeable, Mrs Yeobright severe and self-reliant, and Thomasin, ultimately, patient and serene. A clear distinction is drawn between those characters in revolt, who hate the heath (Eustacia and Wildeve), and those more submissive individuals who come to terms with life on Egdon. The discontented Eustacia and Wildeve die in their desperate attempt to escape from the hated environment. So, in a sense, the heath triumphs. But it would probably be a mistake to infer from this that Hardy is in any way celebrating the affirmation of the old order exemplified by the heath; he indicates pretty clearly the limitations of the life of those characters (Clym, Venn, and Thomasin) who submit to the heath. Still, at least it can be said that these characters are, in the end, not unhappy, and are no doubt wise in acquiescing in circumstances which they are powerless to alter. Venn and Thomasin who secure contentment together, offer, in their marriage, what little hope this tragic novel contains.

One attribute of most of the main characters that strikes the reader is their astounding selfishness. With the exception of Diggory and Thomasin they are all egoists, immersed in their own aspirations and uninterested in the wishes of others. It is not fanciful to regard this egoism as nourished by their environment; isolation encourages the characters to affirm their own values without regard to anybody else's. In a very practical way, too, the loneliness of life on the heath encourages the intensifying and prolonging of quarrels which, in a more normal milieu, might quickly blow over. After the estrangement between Mrs Yeobright and her son and daughter-in-law, both the mother and Clym long for reconciliation, and Eustacia is at least not unwilling to make things up. The distances of the heath, which prevent casual meetings or visits, are a major factor in delaying efforts at peace-making, and in causing Mrs Yeobright's effort to restore good relations to end in catastrophe.

Some aspects of the novel suggest that Hardy, in developing it, may have deviated from his original plans regarding it. The ideas of social restlessness and human aspiration are raised in a manner that interests the reader, but these concepts are not fully developed, becoming in the end subordinate to the simpler tragic romance of Clym, Eustacia, and Wildeve. There are some indications, too, that Hardy was attempting, in novel form, a tragedy on the old heroic model of the Greek tragic drama. In staging all the action on the heath, he probably had in mind the old classical requirement of "unity of place" (the rule that, in a play, all the scenes should take place in the one location); and, in his depiction of the tragic deaths of, first, Mrs Yeobright and, secondly, Eustacia and Wildeve, he seems to have been imitating the many classical plays in which characters are destroyed either through a tragic flaw in their dispositions or by the cruelty of a malevolent fate. The impression of an attempt at a classical tragedy is strengthened by the weight of classical allusion in the novel, much of this being heaped on the character of Eustacia; in addition, the author constantly strains towards a prose of epic-type grandeur. But, in the end, Hardy's attempt at a heroic simplicity is foiled by the very modern and complex characters whom he has created. In their restlessness, vague aspirations and changeability, which put them at variance with each other, they are too essentially nineteenth-century persons to form part of a classical tragedy, and the book emerges as a study of modern life against a timeless background.

Assessment of plot

The plot of the novel must be viewed largely as the working-out of Hardy's concept of a fatality that thwarts all human efforts to secure happiness. The central episode of the book, the closed door, an incident that leads directly to the later disasters, is the most notable example of this fatality in action. A number of factors, which the reader can easily list, combine to result in this incident, and all these are examples of a malevolent chance operating. The reader may be disposed to criticize this cumulation of unlucky factors as too coincidental, but the piling-up of unfortunate circumstances should be viewed simply as an illustration of Hardy's fatalism. Certainly, one can agree with those who point out that the novel does not illustrate total determinism; both the incident itself and its subsequent consequences *could* have been avoided, given more intelligence and generosity on the part of those involved. But Hardy has depicted with very convincing skill the circumstances which make the closed door incident a kind of tinder to gunpowder: the estrangement between Clym and his mother, and the building-up of bad feeling and suspicion between Mrs Yeobright and Eustacia; given these conditions, the tragedy of the closed door seems unavoidable.

It is also true that a certain convincing inevitability of dissension arises from the very nature of the characters. The instability of Wildeve, who fluctuates between Eustacia and Thomasin; the incompatibility of the aims of Clym and Eustacia;

the pride and hot temper of both Eustacia and Mrs Yeobright: all these attributes make the final catastrophes seem impossible to avoid.

As always in Hardy, some of the details of the plot strain the reader's credulity. The sudden appearances of the apparently omniscient Diggory Venn, who constantly springs up to protect Thomasin's interests in the style of a secret service agent, are impossible to credit. The most extreme instance of this incredible intelligence work is the gambling episode, in which Mrs Yeobright's hundred guineas are won, first by Wildeve from the wretched Cantle, and then from Wildeve by Venn. Apart from the unlikelihood of Venn's being there at all, one must point out that the mathematical odds against such extreme swings of gambling fortune are millions to one.

Characters

Hardy has left it on record that he intended Clym to be the chief character of the novel (as the title indicates), but in reality it is Eustacia who steals the book. The author makes very deliberate attempts to romanticize and glorify Eustacia. Much emphasis is laid on her beauty; she is described successively as 'queen of night', 'queen of the solitude', and 'the raw material of a divinity', and we are told that, given the right trimmings or background, she could ressemble Artemis, Athena, or Hera. She is frequently depicted romantically at a distance, silhouetted against the heath, and images of fire are constantly associated with her.

In spite of all this, however, it is very noticeable that, when Eustacia herself speaks and acts, she ceases to be an idealized heroine, and becomes instead merely a fatally bored and discontented young woman. Much of her dissatisfaction is understandable; she is forced to live a life of unnatural isolation in an uncongenial environment. Unfortunately, her discontent is wholly negative; she never has any sensible ideas for improving her state, and rejects Venn's offer of a post in Budmouth simply because it would involve doing some work.

Eustacia's yearnings for luxury, grandeur, and great loves are absurd, and cause her to confuse dreams with reality. This confusion leads her both to an unsatisfactory affair with Wildeve, whom she really knows is not worth the emotion she expends on him, and to a disastrous marriage with Clym, whom she mistakenly views as a heroic visitant who will speedily transport her to the delights of Paris. Clym disappoints her in this, but one suspects that, even if he had carried out her wishes, Eustacia would soon have found some cause for complaint in Parisian bourgeois life. The root of her discontent lies within herself, and she strongly resembles Emma Bovary, the heroine of Flaubert's novel, in her inability to come to terms with ordinary life. For the real Clym, with his altruistic aspirations and his difficulties with weak eyesight, she has no sympathy and little sincere affection.

Why then does Eustacia, in spite of her glaring defects, still arouse a great deal of sympathy? Possibly because she is young, immature, and lonely; because she has a concept of greatness even if no idea how to attain it; and, above all, because, like so many Hardy characters, she suffers greatly through her own weaknesses. Hardy correctly indicates that her tragic death, occurring as it does when her youth and beauty still have power to stir the imagination, is in many ways a merciful ending for her.

Yeobright, obviously intended to be mainly a fine man and a sympathetic character, emerges as a saddening study of a botched life. His aims are noble, but in the end he attains no more than uncomplaining acquiescence, illustrated by the manner in which he becomes absorbed into the heath's flora and fauna while working as a humble furze-cutter. He himself is at home on the heath, but his very content makes him strangely blind to the miserable nature of the existence which he provides for a high-spirited young wife. He is presented as a man of strong affections, yet he is very ineffectual in his handling of the two women he loves (Eustacia and his mother). He quarrels easily, is slow to attempt the reconciliations which he really desires, and indulges in useless excessive remorse when the objects of his love are dead. His tragedy is that he wishes to live among the heath-dwellers, but is educated beyond them; at the same time, he aspires to philosophy, yet has not quite the intellectual grasp needed to attain it.

The character of Wildeve, although not very developed, is an acute study of a man who trifles, both in his affections and in his career. He is neither just nor kind to Thomasin, and it is typical of him that he finally marries her partly in order to spite Eustacia. He is incapable of giving or receiving lasting happiness, because he always tires of the possessed and longs for the unattainable; Eustacia becomes desirable again to him when she is married to another man. He tends to be the more passive character in his dealings with her, and it seems appropriate that he should finally be led to disaster by her, an end foretold by the image of the moth and the lighted candle associated with him. (See Book IV, Chapter IV).

Diggory Venn is an exceptionally interesting figure. As the practitioner of a dying trade, he to some extent represents the continuity of the traditions of the heath. He is introduced to us by a sharp visual picture at the beginning of the novel, and he carries continually with him an atmosphere of strangeness, the result both of his bizzarre appearance and of his detective work. Still, he is the only character who consistently thinks of anybody else's welfare, and also the sole individual who really makes a success of life. It is a little difficult to understand why the docile Thomasin, who is not depicted as a young woman of much personality, exerts such a powerful hold on him, but, at all events, Venn deserves his final happiness with her, although this was not the ending that Hardy himself thought artistically right.

Mrs Yeobright is a difficult character to assess. Older critics have often admired her integrity, family pride, and strong maternal affection. Yet, though she loves Clym, she is sometimes harsh to him, and, because of her possessive love for him, she is grudging and unwelcoming to Eustacia. Family pride and love of respectability also make her unjust and unkind to Thomasin over the failed wedding.

Narrative style

The artistry with which Hardy builds up his story is impressive. The narrative develops at a slow, unhurried pace. The dominant environment is first firmly set by the chapter describing the heath. Then Captain Vye is introduced as he speaks to Venn, who is conveying the disappointed Thomasin back home. The reader's attention is next shifted to the immobile figure of Eustacia silhouetted against the heath, and from her to the country people lighting their bonfires. All these visual pictures are presented as if from the viewpoint of an observer of the scene.

Then, through the conversation of the rustics, we learn the important facts about Thomasin's and Wildeve's relationship. In this way, the reader is cleverly introduced to some of the chief characters and the main issues.

The prevailing style of *The Return of the Native,* formerly much admired, is now often criticized as pretentious and over-ambitious. One extract which is now often termed theatrical is the opening chapter describing Egdon Heath. Here is a passage from this chapter:

> It was a spot which returned upon the memory of those who loved it with an aspect of peculiar and kindly congruity. Smiling champaigns of flowers and fruit hardly do this, for they are permanently harmonious only with an existence of better reputation as to its issues than the present. Twilight combined with the scenery of Egdon Heath to evolve a thing majestic without severity, impressive without showiness, emphatic in its admonitions, grand in its simplicity.

There are obvious faults in this passage. Hardy is, in it, frequently piling up adjectives which, when examined, do not convey any precise meaning. The reader is not helped to form a clear picture of the heath by being told that it is "majestic without severity" (this is very vague; besides, the heath elsewhere *is* shown to be severe), or "emphatic in its admonitions" (who or what is Egdon supposed to be admonishing?). Much of the writing is laboured and cumbersome; "an aspect of peculiar and kindly congruity" or "an existence of better reputation as to its issues than the present" are examples of phrases whose meaning could have been better expressed more simply. Yet it would be a mistake to write off the description of the heath as a total failure. For all its over-writing, the chapter as a whole does leave in the mind the picture of a lonely, mysterious, prehistoric place, and therefore clearly establishes the dominant mood of the novel.

Similarly, in describing Eustacia (Book 1, Chapter VII), Hardy is often pretentious and imprecise. He is much better when he is depicting his heroine through her own words or actions. Consider, for example, the following paragraph:

> Thus she was a girl of some forwardness of mind, indeed, weighed in relation to her situation among the very rearward of

thinkers, very original. Her instincts towards social non-conformity were at the root of this . . . she hated Sundays when all was at rest, and often said they would be the death of her . . . To relieve the tedium of this untimely day she would overhaul the cupboards containing her grandfather's odd charts and other rubbish, humming Saturday night ballads of the country people the while. But on Saturday nights she would frequently sing a psalm, and it was always on a week-day that she read the Bible, that she might be unoppressed with a sense of doing her duty.

The first two sentences of this passage are mere cumbersome phrases which convey little precise impression; in contrast, the last two sentences are vivid and revealing because they relate exactly what Eustacia *does*. They succeed in conveying, in a very brief space, Eustacia's innate perverseness of disposition.

The dialogue of the novel also shows at different times both Hardy's strengths and weaknesses. Sometimes the conversations sound theatrical and unnatural, and as though they had been copied from third-rate melodrama. Examples are the conversation between Thomasin and Wildeve after the cancellation of the wedding (Book I, Chapter V), the quarrel between Mrs Yeobright and Eustacia (Book IV, Chapter I), and the quarrel between Eustacia and Clym (Book V, Chapter III). On the other hand, the novel also contains many examples of good dialogue, where the speakers express themselves simply and naturally. Take, for instance, the following conversation between Eustacia and Wildeve early in the novel (Book I, Chapter IX):

'. . . Eustacia, how we roved among these bushes last year, when the hot days had got cool, and the shades of the hills kept us almost invisible in the hollows!'

She remained in moody silence till she said, 'Yes; and how I used to laugh at you for daring to look up to me! But you have well made me suffer for that since.'

'Yes, you served me cruelly enough until I thought I had found one fairer than you. A blessed find for me, Eustacia.'

'Do you still think you found somebody fairer?'

'Sometimes I do, sometimes I don't. The scales are balanced so nicely that a feather would turn them.'

'But don't you really care whether I meet you or whether I

don't?' she said slowly.

'I care a little, but not enough to break my rest,' replied the young man languidly. 'No, all that's past. I find there are two flowers where I thought there was only one . . .'

The first sentence spoken here by Wildeve has a poetic vein which reminds us that Hardy is often a poet in words even in his prose fiction; but the exchange is chiefly noteworthy for the remarkable self-knowledge of Wildeve, who can analyse his own feelings very accurately, and for the searching questions of Eustacia, who at heart knows how little her lover really cares for her. The unembellished directness of this dialogue shows a liking for honesty that strikes the reader as very modern.

The critic is also very forcibly struck by the picture given of the enduring life of the heath. Almost all the significant action of the novel takes place out of doors there; the heath is the scene of numerous meetings, both planned and unplanned, and of many other incidents. Much of the action takes place by night, when the little fires lit by the country people, and by Eustacia, form a distinctive feature of the environment. Hardy often reveals a poet's ability to integrate the characteristics of the heath with the individual's state of mind at any given time. Thus, in Book IV, Chapter II, Clym's state of contented acquiescence in his fall to the lowly status of furze-cutter is indicated by the manner in which he forms part of the natural flora and fauna of the place. The clump of battered, worn-out trees near Clym's house, in whose shade Mrs Yeobright sits down to rest after her journey, mirrors the exhausted condition of Mrs Yeobright herself (Book IV, Chapter V). The continuity of life on the heath is shown by the country people's traditional pastimes, such as the mummers' performance and the dancing festival, both of which are significant to the plot, while Hardy also skilfully uses the witchcraft practised by Susan Nonsuch against Eustacia to increase the atmosphere of fatality built up towards the end of the novel.

Hardy, however, very clearly indicates the limitations of the rustics in his novels. These are epitomized by the foolishness of Christian Cantle, who loses Mrs Yeobright's hundred guineas to Wildeve through optimistic gambling. Against Cantle's irresponsibility, however, must be set the steadiness of Charley, the young lad who is devoted to Eustacia. As always, the talk of the country people is pithy and humourous.

The Return of the Native is a very ambitious novel, in which Hardy's reach perhaps exceeds his grasp. It does not quite succeed in reaching the level of grand tragedy aimed at; still, it does succeed in presenting an absorbing picture of modern and fallible people involved in complex relationships in an unusual and interesting environment.

4

The Mayor of Casterbridge

As though to emphasize that Hardy's career as a writer shows no consistent pattern of development, the publication of *The Return of the Native* was followed by the writing of three works which are undeniably minor.

The first of these, *The Trumpet-Major* (1880), is interesting because it is Hardy's only attempt at the historical novel; in the main, it is a successful example of the genre. Set in the England of the Napoleonic Wars, dominated by the threat of invasion, the book is primarily an entertainment, with an attractive gallery of comic characters, although the personality and fate of John Loveday, the trumpet-major of the title, introduce a deeper note into what is mainly a very light-hearted tale.

A Laodicean (1881) is in many ways Hardy's most disappointing novel. It begins very promisingly with a heroine (the Laodicean of the title) who hesitates between the new industrial world represented by her wealthy and successful father who has left her a fortune, and the old traditional values of the now impoverished aristocracy epitomized by the ancient castle in which she lives. Unfortunately, the book soon degenerates into a mixture of boring travelogue and a crude melodrama centred on a sinister young villain who is the illegitimate son of one of her suitors. It was probably mainly because Hardy was seriously ill at the time of writing that he failed to develop the original creative ideas of the book; most of it was dictated to Mrs Hardy from his sick-bed.

It is difficult to give a summary verdict on *Two on a Tower* (1882). There is an elusive charm in this book, whose plot centres on the love affair and secret marriage between a young lady of the manor and an even more youthful astronomer who studies his science in a tower situated on her estate. The stellar background to the story is unusual and interesting, and the love between the pair is characterized by a touching innocence and devotion; but the very limited range of the novel, much of whose action takes place in the circumscribed area of the tower, effectively restricts this novel to the minor category.

Hardy returned to more significant work with *The Mayor of Casterbridge,* published in 1886, a powerful and moving account of the rise and fall of its central character, Michael Henchard, the Mayor of the title. The book is set in the country town of Casterbridge, and the life, politics, and rivalries of the town form an important aspect of this novel.

Themes

The dominating theme of the book is the fate of its central character. Michael Henchard is the most vital and dominating male character in all Hardy's fiction; unlike most of Hardy's heroes, who are poor and obscure, he becomes a man of substance and reaches a position of importance in the world of local politics. His subsequent fall has something of the quality of an ancient classical tragedy, an impression which is heightened by the emphasis given to the old Roman character of Casterbridge. A nemesis seems to be pursuing Henchard, and he has been freely likened to Oedipus or Lear because of the unrelenting manner in which fate heaps successive blows upon him, and completes his ruin in spite of his dogged efforts to avert disaster.

Henchard's fall may be attributed to two major factors. The first is a single amoral act committed by him twenty years before the main action of the story begins: the auction of his wife at a fair in a moment of drunkenness and bad temper. This act, representing as it does the reduction of a human being to a piece of merchandise, infringes the standards of civilized society, and the repercussions of it prove to be inescapable, in spite of Henchard's repentance of his folly. The wife-sale effectively ensures Henchard's isolation for most of his life, since he cannot marry for fear that the auctioned Susan is still living; it is the cause of his bitter misery when he finds that the girl whom he cherishes as his daughter, Elizabeth-Jane, is not after all his child; finally, when the act is revealed over twenty years later by an original witness of it, the disclosure effects Henchard's disgrace and social ruin in an outraged society, and, by finally estranging the woman whom he is now courting (Lucetta), removes from him any hope either of marital happiness or of financial rescue.

The second cause of Henchard's ruin is simply his own character. 'Character is Fate,' quotes Hardy in this novel, and nemesis works unerringly through Henchard's own glaring defects. A blundering over-reacher, he is characterized by volcanic passions, violent jealousy, and a total lack of diplomacy and of any spirit of conciliation. These attributes lose him the favour of the influential citizens who made him Mayor, and cause him to enter into an unnecessary commercial war with Farfrae, the young rival whom he formerly befriended. A mixture of sheer bad luck and of a credulous addiction to fortune-telling cause Henchard to be the loser in the struggle; he is declared bankrupt, and his business and his house are bought by his successful rival, who also becomes Mayor.

The combined disasters which overwhelm Henchard — social, emotional, political, and commercial failure all united — make this a tale of appalling tragedy, and the effect of suffering of great magnitude is merely heightened by the defiant courage and pride with which Henchard faces disaster.

Since the personality of Henchard dominates the book, the novel's main tone is deeply and despairingly pessimistic; Henchard dies lonely, unloved, and unreconciled. The gloom is, however, lightened a little by the eventual happiness and prosperity of the young people in the story: Elizabeth-Jane, Henchard's supposed daughter, and the Scot, Farfrae. Compared with the volcanic Henchard, these two are quiet, rather shadowy figures (although Elizabeth-Jane often reveals surprising reserves of strength), but both show how steady, patient effort can secure its reward. Farfrae is, after all, when he sets up in business as a competitor to Henchard, faced with the same set of commercial and social circumstances as the older man; he merely, because of his steadier character, makes better use of them. The novel shows virtually an "hour-glass" plan, Farfrae's fortunes rising in proportion to the decline in those of Henchard.

A third theme in the novel is the need for patient acceptance of adversity. It is part of Hardy's message that Fate cannot be avoided, and his grim belief is that life brings more trials than joys; yet at the same time he often shows how the worst of

Fortune's knocks may be made more endurable by a spirit of quiet acceptance, mixed with courage and humour. Elizabeth-Jane, during the period when both Henchard and Farfrae neglect her, and Lucetta makes use of her, demonstrates the truth of this teaching; her calm, serene philosophy at least makes her situation bearable. This fact is one which the proud, hot-tempered, impatient Henchard never learns. Although he shows some good qualities in his ruin, notably his stoicism and his honest efforts to pay his creditors, he generally merely increases his own misery through his bitterness and envy. He quarrels with Farfrae, who has made sincere efforts to help him by giving him a job in his business, and by buying some of his auctioned furniture in order to restore it to him; he alienates Elizabeth-Jane's affection by selfishly trying to appropriate it all for himself and driving away the girl's real father, Newsom; he invites the rough treatment which he receives by making a foolish exhibition of himself at the visit of the Royal Personage.

Assessment of plot

The Mayor of Casterbridge is the most carefully and successfully plotted of all Hardy's major novels. The author's invention never flags, and the narrative is constantly moving. The result is a strong story, giving a sense of constant creative power. Indeed, a minor criticism of the book might be that the amount of incident in it is almost excessive.

Hardy in this novel is particularly good at springing well-planned surprises on the reader. The question of Elizabeth-Jane's parentage is skilfully handled, and the revelation that she is not, after all, Henchard's daughter comes as a very real shock. Similarly, the sudden marriage of Lucetta and Farfrae is cleverly concealed until it makes the maximum impact by destroying at a single blow Henchard's hopes both of marriage and of financial rescue.

One main criticism of the plot that probably occurs to every reader is that the cumulation of blows of ill-fortune on Henchard seems to be excessive. Everything strikes at about the same time: his financial ruin through credulous gambling on the harvest, the loss of his hopes of Lucetta, the social disgrace incurred through the exposure of the wife-sale, and the discovery that Elizabeth-Jane is not his own child. Is it not all too coincidental? Possibly; but it seems to be a part of Hardy's philosophy that troubles never come singly, and, certainly, all Henchard's misfortunes can be convincingly traced to his own character and actions.

Some incidents, however, do seem in themselves far-fetched. The wife-sale, on which the whole story depends, undeniably puts something of a strain on the reader's credulity. Of course, it is true, as some critics point out, that such sales were historically not unknown, and that Hardy has the support of established records for the incident, but it is so bizarre and uncivilized a transaction that it remains difficult for it to carry full artistic conviction. Hardy certainly uses all his narrative skill in his endeavour to make the strange episode believable (as will be described later).

There are a number of other incidents that take a good deal of swallowing: the appearance of the furmity-woman in court before Henchard, and her exposure of the wife-auction over twenty years after the event; the reappearance of Lucetta in Henchard's life, just after his wife Susan conveniently dies; the return of the sailor, Newsom, hitherto presumed dead. Clearly none of these events is impossible, but the perceptive reader is conscious of Hardy's hand loading the fates against his unlucky central character. Yet, in a sense these somewhat unlikely coincidences matter little, because the character of Henchard himself is such a vital, dynamically alive creation that it carries the story along through all the incidents of the plot, likely or unlikely. Imaginative belief in Henchard himself compels belief in what happens to him. As one critic expresses it, "The plot may creak, but Henchard lives".

Characters

Henchard is the complete antithesis of the good, mild, somewhat passive male central characters found in so many of Hardy's novels. Vital, energetic, unreflecting, his personality completely dominates the book; his creator sums him up well as 'a vehement and gloomy being'. He is the slave of the passions of the moment, as unthinking often as a child or an animal. This predominance of the emotional in his make-up is reponsible for his violent swings from love to hate. He cherishes Elizabeth-Jane when he thinks she is his daughter, but subjects her to harsh usage when he discovers her real parentage, which a more reasonable man might have reflected was no fault of hers. He gives warm affection at first to the attractive young Scot, Farfrae, but jealousy turns his regard into an undeserved hatred.

A salient characteristic of Henchard — a grave defect in a public man — is that he always expresses his true feelings, unrestrained by tact, by consideration for others, or by expediency. As a result, he clashes with people who, more tactfully handled, could have been his friends or helpers. He virtually drives Farfrae from his employment in spite of the young Scot's usefulness to him, initiates a commercial war which his young rival in no way desires, and discourages his courtship of Elizabeth-Jane which, if it had resulted in marriage, could have converted Farfrae from a rival into a partner and supposed son-in-law. Again, Henchard tries to ride roughshod over his employee Abel Whittle by ordering him to set off to work half-clothed, and by his tactlessness he offends the same Council members who, impressed by his energy, originally made him Mayor. 'Loving a man or hating him,' comments Hardy, 'his diplomacy was as wrong-headed as a buffalo's.'

This is not to say that Henchard is incapable of good actions; he is, but paradoxically, these often recoil to his disadvantage, or at least do not benefit him, because the recipients are those who are without influence. He tries to make amends for the original wife-sale by re-marrying Susan twenty years later; the only result for Henchard of this act of atonement is to lower his standing in Casterbridge through his union with so humble a person. 'A poor twanking woman like her,' comments one observer of the wedding. '— tis a godsend for her, and hardly a pair of jumps or night-rail to her name.' Henchard may bully Abel Whittle, but it is also revealed that he keeps Whittle's poor old mother in coals and snuff; old Mrs Whittle's opinion of the Mayor, however, is not one that counts in the town.

Although often kind of heart, Henchard is basically a man who grossly over-estimates himself, as his wrong-headed trade war with Farfrae, a man who has a far more astute judgement, clearly reveals. In many of his actions can be seen a virtual impulse towards self-destruction, an obstinate persistence on paths of conduct that can lead only to ruin. Always an isolated man,

Henchard, through his behaviour, is fundamentally at war with society, and society destroys him. In the end, he resembles a bull which has been tamed for the pleasure or edification of the spectators, a fate which Henchard's own bull-taming incident (in which he shows no lack of courage) serves to symbolize.

Henchard in his ruin is a saddening picture: rancorous, quarrelsome, envious. There is a profound pessimism in the ending of the novel in which he dies (virtually because he no longer wishes to live), alone and unreconciled, leaving behind him the bitter will in which he directs, among other things, that Elizabeth-Jane is not to be told of his death and that no man is to remember him. It is true that a glimmer of light shines in Henchard's contrition for his deception of Elizabeth-Jane and in his efforts to atone for this, yet here, his penitence itself is excessive and somewhat morbid. Henchard, whether behaving well or ill, is always immoderate and unbalanced in his actions.

In many ways, Henchard's conduct represents an abuse of the limited free will which is all that Hardy's philosophy allows to Man. It seems so obvious that he could have avoided his worst disasters by being more sensible and moderate, and that he could have taken the worst edge off his final poverty and disgrace by patient resignation. But part of the deep gloom of this novel is due to the underlying doubt expressed as to how real a choice Henchard has to act other than he does. The free will is almost non-existent; Henchard is virtually incapable of moderating his emotions or regulating his actions. The reader has a sense that even his character is not his fault, and so the book is permeated with the hopelessness of determinism.

In spite, however, of his grave faults, Henchard manages to retain the reader's sympathy. One reason for this is that he is very human in his affections and dislikes, and obviously very vulnerable to the disappointments of life. One's feelings go out to him in his fall because Henchard himself feels the disaster so bitterly. And, even at the lowest ebb of his fortunes, he retains a vision of the good, a sense of right and wrong. He is subject to the worst and meanest temptations: to kill Farfrae when he has him at his mercy during their fight; to expose Lucetta's past to her husband; later, to alienate Farfrae from Elizabeth-Jane, and so keep her to himself, by exposing the fact that she is, legally, nobody's child. It is to Henchard's credit that he retains enough moral sense to resist these temptations.

Farfrae is clearly planned to represent a complete contrast in temperament to Henchard, just as his steady progress upwards in life shows the reverse pattern to Henchard's fall. Light-hearted, cheerful, sociable, he is as understandably popular as Henchard is disliked. He has many solid, if limited good qualities, and it is easy to see why he commands enough influence to be made Mayor. He is a sensible, orderly man of business (unlike Henchard, who is totally unorganized), receptive to new ideas for instance on machinery (as Henchard is not), cautious and safe in his buying. Often, he reveals very genuine human decency, as when he stands up to his employer Henchard in the affair of Abel Whittle and his breeches, or when he makes sincere efforts to help Henchard in his ruin by giving him a job and offering him rooms in his house.

Farfrae's chief defect is that he is shallow. Untouched by inner conflict himself, he is unaware of it in others. He lacks the imagination to understand Henchard's original strong affection for himself, or to comprehend the older man's misery in his fall. His own emotions are always well under control; his affection swings easily from Elizabeth-Jane to the superficially charming Lucetta, then later back to the younger woman again.

Two incidents, in particular, tend to make one dislike Farfrae. One is that, as Mayor, he refuses Henchard's harmless request to form part of the reception committee to receive the Royal Personage, because he sees that the Council do not want the disgraced ex-Mayor. The other is that, at the end of the story, Farfrae calls off the search for Henchard that he and Elizabeth-Jane are carrying out, because otherwise they risk having to stay away from home for the night, and "that will make a hole in a sovereign". Meanness is not an engaging attribute.

Elizabeth-Jane is a quietly attractive character, with an unusual strength and serenity for so young a woman. Experience of earlier adversity has taught her not to have any wildly inflated expectations of life; her head is not turned by her temporary spell of prosperity in Henchard's home, and she reveals philosophy and humour during the neglect she experiences in Lucetta's household. Although understandably indignant more than once at Henchard's treatment of her, she is kind to him after his fall, and her affection is the one bright gleam in Henchard's dark life. She attains a deserved happiness — admittedly of the subdued variety — at the end of the novel, and, characteristically, is shown as using her own knowledge of life to teach others how to make limited opportunities endurable.

Artistically, Elizabeth-Jane carries out several important functions in the story. Much of the narrative is from her point of view, and it is as the perceptive observer of events close to her that she is chiefly prominent. However, in her youthfulness, hopefulness, and eventual happiness, she forms a much-needed foil to Henchard, whose nature and fortunes are alike so dark that, if unrelieved, they would threaten to make the book unbearably gloomy. In herself, and in her sane attitude to life, Elizabeth-Jane serves to underline the wrong-headedness of so many of Henchard's attitudes. Yet she herself, paradoxically, is used by the nemesis that is pursuing Henchard; probably the worst moment, emotionally, in his whole life is that in which he learns that Elizabeth-Jane is not, after all, his daughter.

The character of Lucetta is little but a stock picture of an ageing siren with a shadowy past. Her selfishness and shallowness are clearly depicted, but otherwise she has few noteworthy attributes, and the conventional nature of this portrait is an example of Hardy's limited skill in depicting the more cultivated woman.

Environment

The environment deserves a brief reference, since the milieu of Casterbridge is central to the story. The novel gives a very authoritative picture of a country town, an evolving social organism, and also of the agricultural world in the time before the repeal of the Corn Laws. The rural character of the town is emphasized; its streets lead straight into the country, without any intervening suburbs; vans filled with country produce occupy the streets. It is on agriculture that the entire town lives, so that the conversation even at the dinner parties of the professional classes is about the harvest. The centre of the town is the market place, and it is no accident that so much of the action of the novel takes place in or near this spot.

What is striking in this book, which has been termed by one

critic a novel of character in relation to environment, is how little real connection Henchard has with the social organism. He has been elected Mayor of the town—in itself perhaps an indication of the limitations of Casterbridge life—but he is noticeably isolated in it. In all his years of upward progress, he does not seem to have made a single friend in Casterbridge—no doubt because his attention is too firmly fixed on his own personal ambition.

The lay-out and social divisions of the town are described with unusual thoroughness. It is generally a prosperous place; but near the houses and inns of the more affluent are places like 'The Three Mariners,' frequented by the poor workpeople, such as Christopher Coney and his friends; the average wage of men such as these is eight shillings a week. Below this group again is the poorest and most vice-ridden quarter of the town: Mixen Lane, in which all kinds of ne'er-do-wells take refuge, with its tavern, 'Peter's Pence'. The old Roman character of the town is also stressed, possibly in an effort to emphasize how classical is the tragedy of Henchard's fall. Old Roman skeletons are often found, and the Ring, or amphitheatre, remains as a place for clandestine meetings or the hatching of intrigues. It is never, because of its sombre character, chosen as the meeting place of happy lovers, so that when Henchard meets the returned Susan there, it is perhaps an omen of future ill-fortune.

Hardy's artistry is revealed at its most skilful in this novel. There is a frequent use of surprise: for instance, in the whole question of Elizabeth-Jane's parentage, and in lesser incidents such as the occasion when Farfrae first appears to Lucetta when she is expecting Henchard. The opening scene of the book, in which Henchard, with his wife and child, is travelling towards the fair at Weydon-Priors, is a magnificent introduction, in which nothing is hurried, and in which the figures of the three travellers have a timeless quality.

Henchard's isolation is already forecast in this first scene, in which he is shown as mentally separated from his wife and child. The wife-sale has already been referred to as a difficult episode to make convincing, but Hardy's treatment of it is masterly. Henchard is shown as initiating the idea as a kind of sour joke, then as continuing it through bad temper and the carelessness induced by drink; Susan's acquiescence—the most unbelievable aspect of the whole incident — is explained through pride and weariness of her husband's unappreciative treatment of her. This does not carry entire conviction, perhaps — would not Susan have been equally likely to repudiate the transaction later, when her anger with Henchard had cooled? — but it at least lulls the reader's doubts. The unnatural nature of this trading in human beings is sensitively indicated by Hardy in his pictures of two horses fondling each other outside the auction tent; the satire in the depiction of the affection of the animals for their own kind is obvious; the treatment of each other by human beings forms all too painful a contrast.

Frequently, the book shows a skilful linking of earlier and later episodes, as though to emphasize that Henchard's life, in total, has a distinct unity in spite of the spectacular changes in his fortunes. At the end of his life, as he tramps the country with his tools looking for work as a hay-trusser, he is in exactly the same material position as at the opening twenty years earlier — an ironic comment on the uselessness of all his worldly ambition. Even when he is at the height of his success, his later descent is forecast. Susan and Elizabeth-Jane first see him, through a lighted window, presiding as Mayor over a dinner given to important citizens of the town, and apparently in an impregnable position; but already at this time discontent with him is expressed by the people of Casterbridge on account of the bad bread produced by his bad grain. The image of the bird which flies into the tent at the fair before the wife-sale — giving Henchard time to retreat from his folly if he wished — looks forward to the goldfinch which, over twenty years later, Henchard gives to Elizabeth-Jane as a wedding present, a symbol both of affection and of desired reconciliation.

Style

Stylistically, this is one of Hardy's best books. In both narration and dialogue, there are fewer of the cumbersome circumlocutions that so frequently mar his style; possibly the high incidence of action helps to keep the narrative moving, and the dialogue crisp and purposeful.

The rustic chorus is very important in *The Mayor of Casterbridge*. For once, its actions contribute significantly to the plot, notably in the skimmity-ride, which causes the death of Lucetta, and in the dilatory behaviour of Abel Whittle, the cause of a near-quarrel between Henchard and Farfrae. In addition, the ordinary people are in this book more shrewd and outspoken, and less self-deprecating than elsewhere. Many of their comments have to be taken seriously: for instance, the verdicts on Henchard's marriage to Susan, or Christopher Coney's pointed enquiry after Farfrae's singing of sentimental Scots songs, 'What did ye come away from yer own country for, young maister, if ye be so wownded about it?' The work-people are depicted as hardworking and good-humoured, but as not free from both envy and greed; Farfrae loses some of his popularity with them when he rises from poverty to prosperity, and Coney is capable of robbing Susan Henchard's dead body of fourpence; his defence of this is couched in the rustics' usual pithy style. 'Why should death rob life o'fourpence?'

For once, too, the rustics form a true chorus, in the classical manner, commenting on the most fateful events in the lives of the main characters. Sometimes they are given words of a memorable beauty to speak, as in Abel Whittle's narration of Henchard's death, or Mother Cuxsom's summing-up of Susan's death:

> 'Well, poor soul; she's helpless to hinder that or anything now. .
> . . . . . . And all her shining keys will be took from her, and her cupboards opened; and little things a' didn't wish seen, anybody will see; and her wishes and ways will be as nothing!'

The Mayor of Casterbridge may be summed up as an excellent novel, dominated by the vital and always fascinating personality of its central character. The environment in which it is set—the world of local trade, politics, and the doings of a busy country town—is an unusual one for Hardy, and the ability which he has shown in depicting it makes one wish that he had portrayed this more complex type of milieu more often.

5

The Woodlanders

The Woodlanders, published in 1887, marks a return by Hardy from the comparative sophistication of country town life and politics to the simplicity of the true rural world of Wessex, in this case the village of Little Hintock, set in the heart of the woodlands and orchards of the region. The horizons of the inhabitants are bounded by their work in the growing and felling of trees, by the trade in timber, exemplified by George Melbury, and by the apple and cider business, whose representative worker is young Giles Winterborne. The novel expresses, perhaps more comprehensively than any other, Hardy's feeling for the agricultural world, its cohesion and deep loyalties, and its resistance to innovation from outside. The requirements of the triangular romantic story of Winterborne, Grace Melbury (the timber merchant's daughter), and Fitzpiers (the new young doctor of good family), impose upon Hardy a somewhat sentimental form, but the book is mainly a work of orthodox realism, distinctive chiefly for its grasp of the daily unspectacular work in woodlands and orchards.

Themes

One major theme of the book is the invasion of the peaceful, conservative world of the woodlands by outsiders who have no roots in the region, and no real concern for its inhabitants. These invaders are characterized by a sophisticated corruption that contrasts sharply with the unspoiled simplicity and honesty of the best of the natives. The chief invader is the local landowner, Mrs Charmond, a woman who is distinguished from the traditional lady of the manor by the fact that she is a town-bred newcomer, of whom the villagers shrewdly remark, 'She's the wrong sort of woman for Hintock—hardly knowing a beech from a woak.' Mrs

Charmond is an exploiting force, extracting a good income from her woodland property, but giving nothing of help or interest to the community. A second intruder is the clever, but perverse and dilettantish young doctor, Fitzpiers, who lives in Hintock ostensibly as a healer of the sick, but who wastes his time in amateur studies and neglects his practice for his highly unprofessional amours. It is not unnatural that there should be a shallow and theatrical liaison between Mrs Charmond and Fitzpiers; these two poseurs have a great deal in common.

Hardy's customary pessimism suffuses this novel. The agricultural world is shown as having only a limited ability to resist exploitation, both economic and sexual, by the intruders. Winterborne, for example, soon finds out how helpless he is when he clashes with the landowner; the result is that Mrs Charmond deprives him of his small house, and, with it, any hope of marrying Grace. Melbury bitterly resents the slight to his daughter represented by Fitzpiers's neglect of her for Mrs Charmond, but he realizes that the simple honesty of the world he has known does not well equip him to deal with the destroyers of Grace's happiness:

> What could he and his simple Grace do to countervail the passions of those two sophisticated beings — versed in the world's ways, armed with every apparatus for victory? In such an encounter the homely timber-dealer felt as inferior as a savage with his bow and arrows to the precise weapons of modern warfare.

Much of the pessimism of the novel derives from the fact that the main sympathetic characters — Giles, Marty South, Grace Melbury — are well aware of how little power they have to direct events or influence their own destinies. Like so many of Hardy's characters, they can only suffer, to a great degree in silence.

A considerable amount of that class feeling often observable in Hardy makes itself felt in the novel. Giles Winterborne, a sturdy and outspoken representative of the independent yeoman class, sometimes directly expresses his sense of independence, as when he refuses to yield the right of way to Mrs Charmond's carriage when its coachman demands precedence over the heavier timber-wagon that Giles is conducting. Sometimes he is explicit in voicing

his unfavourable opinion of the upper classes, as when he says
bluntly to Grace, who is elated by the honour of a visit to the big
house, 'How can you think so much of that class of people?'—an
unusual viewpoint in a Victorian novel. Much of the class feeling
is, however, conveyed more indirectly through the portraits of Mrs
Charmond and Fitzpiers. Both of these automatically consider
themselves superior, because of station and cultivated mode of
living, to the ordinary village people, but the novel shows that, in
human terms, their assumptions that they are of greater value
than others are groundless. Mrs Charmond is irresponsible as a
landowner, and perverse and insincere in her affections; Fitzpiers
is an unconscientious doctor, an unfaithful husband, and a bad
son-in-law. Both in human relations, and as regards the duties of
their respective stations, the pair are worse, and not better, than
the ordinary inhabitants of Hintock whom they despise.

The novel raises interesting questions of the value of culture
and refinement. Melbury, in wanting a "good" match for Grace,
is actuated mainly by a vulgar wish to acquire status for the
daughter on whose education he has spent so much money, but
Grace's own wishes are more subtle. Her good education has made
her genuinely appreciative of the refinements of cultivated
society; as a result, she looks with distaste upon much of Hintock
life, including the disastrous Christmas party that Winterborne
holds mainly in her honour. Yet much of her culture is also a
veneer, and she retains considerable affection for Giles, and for
some of the Hintock ways. As a result, she hangs uneasily
suspended between two different stations of life. Hardy, although
he privately thought that Grace's concern for status was trivial,
shows a great deal of sympathy for the problem of young people,
especially young women, who are educated beyond their parents'
station in life. However, he certainly comes out, in the book,
resoundingly in favour of the virtues of simple, uncultivated
people, in the contrast which he presents between Giles's genuine,
unembellished virtue and the worthlessness of the refined
Fitzpiers. Grace, through her experience of her cultivated
husband's duplicity and faithlessness, inevitably herself comes to
regard sterling qualities as more important than refinement. Of
course, Hardy is very much "rigging" the whole cultural
argument; it would be hard to imagine two more unimpressive

exponents of the educated life than Fitzpiers and Mrs Charmond.

Along with the culture is raised the question of choice and sexual selection. Grace is apparently free to choose her marriage partner, but only in appearance; in reality, she is so worked upon both by parental pressure and by the assumption of the age that a girl who has just left school will almost immediately marry that she has little real freedom of action. She is almost forced into accepting Fitzpiers, although she herself realizes that the influence which he exerts over her is not a healthy one; her own instinctive preference is for Winterborne. Fitzpiers selects Grace because of a genuine sexual attraction; his mistake is to neglect her for Mrs Charmond — his affair with her is a mere compound of snobbery, nostalgia for youth, and perversity. Mrs Charmond's passion for Fitzpiers is a product of both boredom — she has nothing better to do — and a belief in her own imagination.

An interest in legal questions emerges from the novel. Much is made of the unjust system by which the tenure of houses or cottages from the landowner depends on the life of one single individual. That Giles should lose his house because of old John South's death is an obvious flaw in the whole system of agricultural tenure. Even more striking is the emphasis placed on the divorce question. The law on marriage is shown to be unsatisfactory in that it offers no release from a failed marriage, even where, as in this case, the husband has deserted his wife for another woman. In this novel Hardy is clearly beginning to move towards the view, which he made explicit in *Jude the Obscure*, that a marriage should be subject to dissolution whenever it brings unhappiness to the persons united in it.

Assessment of plot

The basic plot of the novel is perhaps somewhat stereotyped, being mainly a stock situation of infidelity and the triangle pattern of Grace, Fitzpiers, and Winterborne. However, the adult nature of the themes (affection versus social ambition, repentance, possible regeneration, and sacrifice) serve to give a new weight and seriousness to a very old and frequently-used situation. The characters, by their behaviour, raise very important issues.

The first half of the book, leading to Grace's marriage, is the stronger part, because in this section the reader has a sense of plot being determined convincingly by character. Suspense is sustained by the masterly way in which Melbury, who is in a sense the arbiter of Grace's fate, is shown as veering like a weathercock between loyalty to Giles and social ambition for his daughter. The most decisive action in the book, Grace's disastrous marriage to Fitzpiers, is credibly depicted as being the inevitable result of a combination of factors. Not the least of these is Grace's own indecisiveness and hankering for gentility, but it is also shown very convincingly how much Melbury's pressure and Winterborne's own lack of self-assertiveness contribute to her acceptance of Fitzpiers. Giles's failure to take the initiative sufficiently is quite believably shown as resulting both from a diffidence and sense of inferiority that are natural to him, and from the economic weakness of his position.

In the second half of the book Hardy's true creative vitality seems to flag a little, and this part becomes flawed by too much unconvincing incident. Much of the progress of the plot rings true enough. Given Fitzpiers's relations with Mrs Charmond, it is quite believable that Melbury should injure him in a quarrel, and that Fitzpiers, as a result, should leave his father-in-law's house and go to live with Mrs Charmond on the Continent. Still, many of the incidents of this half of the book are undeniably absurd: Grace and Mrs Charmond, who are bitter rivals, huddling together and exchanging confidences when lost in the woods; Fitzpiers appearing in a blood-stained condition at Mrs Charmond's window (how has he managed to walk so far?); Grace caught by the skirt in the man-trap intended for Fitzpiers, and subsequently (now minus her skirt), effecting a reconciliation with her distraught husband. And no critic yet has been able to take seriously Mrs Charmond's lover, the passionate gentleman from South Carolina.

The central action of the latter half of the book is the sacrifice and resultant death of Giles. Many critics have regarded this also as almost absurd in its excess, an instance of too-great suffering endured merely to protect Grace's reputation (even though propriety was a more serious question in the last century than in the present). "No one, neither man nor dog, should have to be that loyal," comments the critic Irving Howe. Yet Giles's act, foolish though it may be, remains a beautiful example of devoted love and unselfishness. Part of his tragedy, however, is the very limited gratitude that Grace is capable of feeling for his sacrifice. There is enormous cynicism in the conclusion of the book, in which Grace, at first mourning Giles, speedily forgets him, and effects a reconciliation with her husband, even though one may grant that this is possibly the sole likely or sensible outcome of the whole affair.

The novel is chiefly distinguished by its sensitive feeling for the true value of the life of the woodlands. Hardy has a poetic sense of the integration into the life of Hintock of those unspoiled characters who, being without personal ambition or snobbery, are content with the woodland and understand it. The chief characters who fit naturally into this life are Giles Winterborne and Marty South. They are utter realists, who get on with the necessary work of woods and orchards; in a sense, each is probably the right mate for the other, for, although Winterborne never thinks of loving the devoted Marty, the pair are shown as being on a level of genuine communion with each other through shared work, as in the tree-planting scene. To Marty is given a power of poetic utterance, as in her final speech, in which she expresses both her deep love for him, and her appreciation of his natural gifts.

'Now, my own, own love,' she whispered, 'you are mine, and only mine; for she has forgot 'ee at last, although for her you died! But I—whenever I get up I'll think of 'ee, and whenever I lie down I'll think of 'ee again. Whenever I plant the young larches I'll think that none can plant as you planted; and whenever I split a gad, and whenever I turn the cider wring, I'll say none could do it like you. If ever I forget your name let me forget home and heaven! . . . But no, no, my love, I never can forget 'ee, for you was a good man, and did good things!'

Marty, in fact, has the same 'intelligent intercourse with Nature' as Giles. She is an almost entirely sympathetic character, in the uncomplaining manner in which she toils far into the night for what, even by the standards of the time, is a beggarly pittance, and in her simple, undeclared love for Winterborne. (Her occasional minor acts of spite, such as taunting Giles in a rhyme painted on his cottage wall with the loss of his house and of Grace, or informing Fitzpiers that Mrs Charmond's apparently luxuriant headpiece is in fact made from hair purchased from herself, merely show that she is capable of natural human jealousy.) After Giles's death, she remains as the exponent of the true woodland life, 'the repository . . . of all the sorrows of the Hintock world,' as one critic expresses it. There is some indication that she was originally intended to be the heroine of the novel; the opening chapters of the book are almost exclusively concerned with her, and much of the action is seen from her viewpoint. In many ways she has more genuine worth than the pampered, would-be genteel Grace. But, if she stands for the Hintock world, she also exemplifies the weakness of its resistance to exploitation, as is indicated by her eventual capitulation, after some show of fight, to the offer of money for her hair.

Giles is also shown as exemplifying the best of country life. Grace, disillusioned because of her husband's infidelity with all that represents culture and gentility, appreciates to the full the healthiness of Giles, which contrasts so forcibly with Fitzpiers's perverse duplicity:

> He looked and smelt like Autumn's very brother, his face being sunburnt to wheat colour, his eyes blue as corn-flowers, his sleeves and leggings dyed with fruit-stains, his hands clammy with the sweet juice of apples, his hat sprinkled with pips, and everywhere about him that atmosphere of cider which at its first return each season has such an indescribable fascination for those who have been born and bred among the orchards. Her heart rose from its late sadness like a released bough; her senses revelled in the sudden lapse back to Nature unadorned. (Chapter XXVIII).

When Giles dies, the loss is seen as communal. Hardy shows the woodlands themselves as mourning their dead cultivator.

Yet although Hardy appreciates to the full the virtues of the natural life of the woodlands, he is not blind to its defects. Many of the village people are coarse and ignorant, and their worst aspects are illustrated by the crude and hoydenish antics of the young village girl, Suke Damson. Disease exists in these woodlands, and it is because of an earlier illness that Giles succumbs to the fever that he catches when subjected to exposure in an inadequate shelter. The life of Marty is in many ways stunted and undeveloped because of poverty and ceaseless toil. Hardy also notices the imperfections of other flora and fauna; these, he implies, indicate the utter indifference of nature to the wellbeing of her products.

> On older trees still than these huge lobes of fungi grew like lungs. Here, as everywhere, the Unfulfilled Intention, which makes life what it is, was as obvious as it could be among the depraved crowds of a city slum. The leaf was deformed, the curve was crippled, the taper was interrupted; the lichen ate the vigour of the stalk, and the ivy slowly strangled to death the promising sapling. (Chapter VII)

It is noticeable that the author presents the natives of the woodlands (Grace, Giles, Melbury and his wife, and Marty) a great deal more convincingly than he does the aliens (Fitzpiers and Mrs Charmond). Hardy can never present an authentic-sounding member of the cultivated classes, and this particular lady of the manor and professional gentleman of good family are as wooden as most of the author's upper-class characters. The dialogue between Mrs Charmond and Fitzpiers has the theatrical artificiality of stock fourth-rate romance. It contrasts very forcibly with the natural, expressive speech of the woodlanders. 'Suppose you talk over my head a little longer, Miss Grace Melbury,' says Giles with a sigh, when Grace is enthusing over Mrs Charmond's unconvincing literary ambitions, and discussing what style of author would best suit her efforts; and in that one satirical phrase Winterborne sums up the nature of the gap between Grace and himself. The comment of Melbury to his wife as they return home after Giles's unsuccessful party similarly conveys the timber-merchant's ambition and his dissatisfaction with Giles as a prospective son-in-law: ' "That's the sort of society we've been asked to meet!" he said. "For us old folk it didn't matter, but for Grace—Giles should have known better." '

Scenes which involve both a woodlander and an alien are often saved by the natural-sounding speech of the native. For instance, in the quarrel at night between Fitzpiers and Melbury, much of what the young doctor says is mere rhetoric, but the scene is redeemed by the authentic quality of Melbury's indignant reproaches. Similarly, in the scene where Fitzpiers and Winterborne discuss Grace, whom the doctor has recently seen for the first time, the dry, satirical observations of Giles contrast forcibly with the mixture of poetic rhapsody and cynical self-analysis that Fitzpiers expresses.

Characters

Some critics have written off the characters of *The Woodlanders* as insipid. It must be admitted that there is a certain lack of obvious force about them. Grace and Giles are both, in their different ways, very diffident, which is one reason why a romance between them never gets going; Fitzpiers is weak rather than evil, and Marty is stoically self-effacing. But the reader with a sensibility to subtle shades of character will find much to interest him in these very different individuals, who show considerable development in the course of the story.

The character of Grace is a very understanding study of sensitivity — a sensitivity so great that it makes her virtually unable to act at all. She obviously prefers Giles to Fitzpiers, but she lacks the strength to enforce her preference. The chief reason for Grace's crippling hesitancy is in fact that she is too deferential to the wishes of her father, which alter with startling frequency; this excessive respect for parental authority tends to make her seem uninteresting. Grace, however, becomes a force to be reckoned with when, at the end of the book, she casts off the authority of both her husband and her father, and becomes, through her sufferings, a self-assured woman who will not be trifled with. By the conclusion she has tamed Fitzpiers and is capable of dealing with him effectively in their renewed marriage relationship.

The main faults of Fitzpiers, exemplified by his affair with Mrs Charmond, have already been referred to. His utter untruthfulness, illustrated by his fluent explanation of the Suke Damson episode, should also be mentioned, and it should be noted that he is a free-thinker. (Hardy, though himself an agnostic, often links unbelief in his characters with moral defects.) The best side of Fitzpiers is linked to his professional skill; he can show himself genuinely self-forgetful when engaged in healing, although he practices his skill in a very desultory way in Hintock. The remorse which he expresses to Grace at the end of the book is sincere, although one cannot help wondering how lasting it will be. Melbury's cynicism may be justified when he comments on Grace's future: "It's a forlorn hope for her; and God knows how it will end!"

However, it would be a mistake to attach too much weight to any of the opinions of Melbury. He is an unimpressive figure, gravely flawed by snobbery, veering uncertainly between a sense of obligation to Giles and a patronizing belief in the young woodlander's social and intellectual inferiority to his daughter. He has one good scene, that in which he makes his sincere and concerned appeal to Mrs Charmond to spare Grace; but for most of the book he is a pathetic blunderer, pushing Grace into her ill-advised marriage, quarrelling unhelpfully with Fitzpiers, foolishly holding out to Grace false hopes of a divorce based merely on the opinion of a local failed lawyer. Melbury is devoted—too devoted—to his daughter, but throughout the story he is perpetually her evil genius.

It is impossible, as one reads the book, not to be frequently impatient with Giles Winterborne. The sterling virtues of Giles are conspicuous and unquestionable, but he is, like so many Hardy heroes, curiously passive and unassertive; a fog of defeat often seems to hang round him. He appears at his best in his own natural environment, as Grace herself appreciates, and, fittingly, it is there that he carries out the great act of unselfish kindness that, in effect, ends his life. In any social situation—at the party, for instance, or in the town of Sherton—his social deficiencies and lack of care for appearances cause him to make a worse impression than he need. It is perhaps inevitable that he should idealize Grace from a distance; the gaps in outlook between them, though based on trivialities, are real, and, in spite of their mutual affection, it is difficult to imagine a satisfactory marriage between the simple, rough-and-ready yeoman and the fastidious cultivated young woman.

Hardy shows great skill and artistry in this book in developing his themes. Hintock is cleverly introduced to the reader with the arrival of the barber, Percomb, in his attempt to buy Marty's hair, and this episode also arouses the reader's interest in Mrs

Charmond. Then, through Marty, interest shifts naturally to Melbury and his daughter. The hair-buying is skilfully made to serve the interests of the plot later in the story, when Marty divulges it by letter to Fitzpiers, and so helps to bring about the quarrel between Fitzpiers and Mrs Charmond and their resultant separation. Interest is also built up in Fitzpiers before the young doctor appears through numerous references to his cleverness, addiction to study, and diabolical nature; Grace is half-disposed to be fascinated by Fitzpiers before she even meets him.

The author's characteristic powers show themselves most fully in the detailed descriptions of the woods, which are masterpieces of detailed observation. Hardy uses much of his imagery to stress the identity of the inhabitants with their environment; the woodlands are represented as mourning the dead Winterborne, and the elm tree which is summarily cut down perhaps symbolizes old John South's life (although the imagery is a little obscure here). The man-trap in which Grace is caught possibly symbolizes the snare of an unhappy marriage.

The rustic chorus plays a very minor part in this novel. There are occasional pithy comments from the villagers on their supposed superiors, not least at the close of the book when Grace's reconciliation with Fitzpiers is under discussion. Creedle, Giles's servant, is humourous and outspoken, especially at the Christmas party. Old Grammer Oliver, who frequently talks very good sense, is original and interesting. But, in general, the ordinary people of Hintock do not enter the narrative much, although the village girls' revels on Midsummer Eve and the sporting of Suke Damson are important to the plot.

The Woodlanders may be summed up as a novel of considerable achievement which is chiefly memorable for its celebration of the simple virtues of the best of the normal community life of the woodlands. It falls below Hardy's finest work because of a degree of insipidity in the main characters, and a certain triviality in their preoccupation with questions of social status; but it nevertheless retains the interest of the reader because of its assured handling of its chief themes, and its sensitive insight into human weakness.

6

Tess of the D'Urbervilles

Following the widespread success of *The Woodlanders,* Hardy published in 1891 a novel which was also syndicated in the latter half of that year in serial form in a number of newspapers. This was *Tess of the d'Urbervilles,* perhaps the author's finest work. It is his most poetically integrated book, and his deep and tender compassion for his unfortunate heroine shines consistently through his writing.

Themes

The most obvious theme of the novel is the undeserved suffering of the beautiful and innocent in a hard world. Tess is a lovely and unspoiled young girl when she leaves her parents' cottage in Marlott to work at the house of her supposed relatives. The rest of the book is a sad and moving chronicle of her suffering, chiefly at the hands of the two men in her life: Alec d'Urberville, who seduces her, and Angel Clare, whom she loves and marries, but who deserts her when he hears of the earlier seduction. The section of the book dealing with Clare's repudiation of Tess is appropriately called 'The Woman Pays', and it is in fact part of Hardy's message to show that, in the nineteenth century, it is the woman who incurs the social stigma for behaviour for which men may be chiefly to blame. Tess's innate disposition is good, but she is taken advantage of; implicitly, Hardy is attacking the Victorian concept of the double standard, by which extra-marital sexual activity by men is condoned as a natural weakness, but if engaged in by women is censured as evidence of vice.

This is not to say that Hardy is in any sense admiring loose or immoral behaviour. On the contrary, his whole point is that Tess is innately innocent, 'a pure woman' as the defiant sub-title of the book makes clear. Purity, in his view, is to be judged by natural disposition and tendencies, not by the mere accidents of Fate which may happen to any individual. Tess in the novel is almost wholly victim; partly the victim of a malevolent chance, and to a considerable extent also the victim of the selfishness of others; this selfishness is exemplified in the unthinking sensuality and acquisitiveness of d'Urberville and in the harsh rigidity of Angel Clare. Tess herself is almost blameless (the question of how far she could have avoided her fate must be considered later).

Hardy also shows very convincingly the manner in which Tess's family contribute to her downfall. The burden which shiftless parents and helpless younger brothers and sisters place on the conscientious Tess is indeed a heavy one, and almost all the disasters that befall her can be attributed in part to her impossible family. The post with the Stoke d'Urbervilles, which leads to her seduction by Alec, is arranged by her parents; the feckless poverty of the family later obliges Tess to give them much of the money provided for her use by Clare, and so forces her to take up the grim agricultural job in which she re-encounters d'Urberville; and it is the homelessness of her family that causes Tess to surrender finally to Alec again. It is small wonder that Hardy indulges in considerable irony about that supposedly sacred unit, the family. Sometimes the irony is overt, as in the passage in which the author describes the helplessness of the Durbeyfield children, and refers satirically to 'Nature's holy plan' (Chapter III); but more often it is implicit, conveyed by his descriptions of the wretched life of the Durbeyfields in their inadequate cottage.

Hardy also illustrates, and uses in his plot, the theme of the break-up of the old agricultural order exemplified in the dispossession of lease and copy holders of cottages (who include the Durbeyfields). It would be a mistake however, to view the book as being chiefly about the ruin of the peasantry, if only because the Durbeyfield parents so obviously represent the peasantry at their worst. However, Hardy certainly succeeds in giving a picture of humble Wessex life from which every illusion has been stripped away; it is hard to conceive of any existence more poverty-stricken, degraded and insecure than that of cottagers such as the Durbeyfields, and this would remain true even if John and Joan Durbeyfield were less shiftless than in fact is the case.

The novel also illustrates the struggle for personal happiness on the part of Tess. Although suffering great adversity, she shows a high degree of resilience, bravely trying to make something of her life in spite of seduction, betrayal, and every kind of harsh treatment. She constantly asserts the right to be human, and to secure a normal human measure of happiness, and she wins the reader's sympathy by her courage and high spirits. In the end, she is inevitably defeated; the cumulation of adverse circumstances proves to be too strong for her.

The defeat and tragic death of Tess — a good and almost blameless person if ever there was one — make this in many ways Hardy's most desolate book. The pessimism that pervades it is more profound even than that of his earlier tragedies, perhaps because Tess is so innocent a victim, guiltless of the more obvious faults of Eustacia or Grace Melbury, and constantly trying to assert the nobler human values. Hardy, when writing this novel, seems to have had no illusions left. The misfortunes which fate heaps upon the unlucky Tess are excessive; the universe is totally uncaring ('Where was Tess's guardian angel?' asks Hardy ironically, in his oblique narration of the seduction); the world is depicted as almost completely harsh and selfish, so that Alec d'Urberville's coarse acquisitiveness and Angel Clare's harsh rigidity are all the more depressing because they are in no way exceptional, but merely part of the universal nature of things.

Assessment of plot

The narrative, which is seen almost entirely through the eyes of Tess, is good because it shows the misfortunes that happen to the heroine, and the frustration of her attempts to do the right thing, as the result of an accumulation of circumstances. For example, Tess genuinely tries several times to confess her past to Angel, she tries to restore relations with him by her visit to his parents, and she does her best to repulse d'Urberville both at the earlier and later stage of their acquaintance. All these efforts fail, mainly owing to the cumulative effects of chance.

One cannot discuss the novel without raising the question of how far the effects of chance could have been circumvented. It is obvious that, in theory, Tess could have acted other than she did, so that the worst of her tragedy was avoided. (She could have continued to resist d'Urberville, she could have confessed her past misadventures to Angel before she married him, and she could have persisted in her efforts to contact his parents.) She does not succeed in doing any of these things because she is not perfect, but human. In spite of the natural goodness of her character, there is observable in her a faint strain of weakness which tends to make her yield ultimately to the pressure of people or events if this is very strong. And, unfortunately, chance seems to be directed always at her weak spot. For example, Tess genuinely wishes to confess to Clare before marrying him, and, being virtually incapable of doing this verbally, informs him of her history by a letter which she pushes under his door. Chance has It that the letter is slipped under the carpet, so that Angel never sees it, thus frustrating Tess's sincere attempts to do the right thing. In theory, of course, she *could* still have confessed verbally to Angel, but the strength of her love, combined with the failure of her past attempt and with Clare's reluctance to hear any recital of her faults, together ensure that she gives up the attempt to be completely honest.

Chance similarly frustrates Tess's attempt to contact Angel's parents. In theory, she should have persevered in her efforts, ignoring the derogatory remarks of the Clare brothers and of Mercy Chant which she happens to overhear. In practice, the rebuff represented by these remarks, coming at a time when Tess is disillusioned and physically weary, proves to be too strong for her persistence.

So one could sum up the reasons for Tess's failures to persist in doing good as: first, a fatality which is difficult to avoid, because it strikes cunningly at the individual's weak spots; and, secondly, Tess's weaknesses themselves. In citing these weaknesses, one is admitting that Tess, although innocent, is not wholly admirable; at many times, because of her weakness, she is more pitiable than admirable. But she retains the reader's love and sympathy because, although fallible, she inclines naturally to the right and good, and makes sincere attempts to adhere to the highest standards, even to her own disadvantage.

The emotional truth of the account of the behaviour of Tess, whose presence dominates the novel, ensures that this is a powerful and convincing novel. It is true that some lesser episodes strike the reader as unbelievable. D'Urberville's temporary conversion to a ranting preacher is incredible, and does not even have the justification of contributing much to the plot; nor, in spite of his persistence, can one believe in his appearance in a smock-frock farming beside Tess at Marlott. A few incidents are absurd: for example, the episode of Clare's carrying the dairymaids across the flooded lane; or Angel's sleep-walking during one night of his honeymoon (even though this does reveal how much Tess's confession has disturbed his mental balance, and therefore has a certain psychological truth).

Perhaps the most controversial episode of all is Angel's reception of Tess's confession to him. Some critics have thought this far-fetched; the irony, they claim, of Angel's treating Tess in this way immediately after his own confession is so great that it is impossible that an intelligent man like Clare should not see it. Although this criticism is understandable, it fails to take into account the prevalence of the Victorian double standard. It was thought natural, if regrettable, that a young man should have sexual lapses in his past life, but shocking and shameful for a woman to have committed the same faults. Clare, in his shocked repudiation of Tess, is merely behaving in a true Victorian manner.

Characters

Tess is the central figure of the entire action of the book, and the novel is brilliant mainly because the portrait of her is a triumph of characterization. Hardy, like many artists, was a man who genuinely loved women and understood the feminine viewpoint, and he portrays Tess with a very sensitive appreciation of her feelings.

His heroine's misfortune is that she is inherently finer than accords with her circumstances; people do not expect such sensitivity from a poor peasant girl. In her situation, her fineness is a disadvantage, since it makes her feel the rough knocks of life too deeply. Her companions at Talbothays Dairy, who instinctively recognize that she is superior to themselves, unintentionally

wound her by recounting what to them is an amusing tale of a
young seducer who, being chased by the girl's angry mother, hides
in a churn. Tess's feelings of distress at this story reveal how deeply
she has felt the tragedy of her own seduction, but Hardy makes it
clear that it is the condemnation of society rather than the mishap
itself that fills her with a painful sense of guilt. 'She had,' he
relates, 'been made to break an accepted social law, but no law
known to the environment in which she fancied herself such an
anomaly.'

This innate refinement makes Tess a complete mystery to the
coarse and acquisitive d'Urberville. 'You are mighty sensitive for a
cottage girl,' he comments in genuine surprise, when she tries to
efface his first kiss by rubbing the spot on her cheek with her
handkerchief. Throughout the novel, he fails to understand her
inner revulsion from him, It is also Tess's own refinement that
causes her to be attracted to Clare, who is outwardly so cultivated,
fastidious, and fine himself. The tragedy is that Angel, with his
high ideals, wrecks Tess's life more thoroughly than even the
crudely selfish d'Urberville.

Tess is characterized by utter devotion and submissiveness to
Angel Clare, whose knowledge and wisdom she over-estimates.
She becomes near-perfect in charity under his recriminations,
submits patiently to being insulted and deserted, and continues to
hope for reconciliation with her insufferable husband for many
months of loneliness. With amazing forbearance, she never once
reminds him of his own self-confessed sexual escapade. Her last
brief letter of bitter reproach to him is understandable; even a
saint would have revolted at Clare's treatment.

For most of the latter half of the novel, Tess struggles bravely, if
sometimes weakly, against a combination of adverse
circumstances. Her final moral collapse represents an inevitable
yielding to a fate which is too strong for her. Hardy expressed his
own view of this in a later comment.

. . . I still maintain that her innate purity remained intact to the
very last; though I frankly own that a certain outward purity
left her on her last fall, I regarded her then as being in the
hands of circumstances, not morally responsible, a mere corpse
drifting with the current to her end.

One reason why this novel is so outstanding is because the action, the states of mind of the characters, and the language are all fused into an integrated poetic whole. The book is the richest in imagery of all Hardy's prose works. The description of the countryside symbolizes Tess's emotional states; the lush beauty of Talbothays in summer mirrors the blooming of Tess during the brief happiness of her courtship, and contrasts with the frozen aspects of the same scene when she re-visits the dairy after her wretched honeymoon. The rootless loneliness of the heroine after Clare's desertion of her is well conveyed by the manner in which she is depicted as tramping the countryside for miles looking for work. The grim barrenness of Flintcomb-Ash and its hard agricultural work suggest the stark misery of Tess's emotional life, while the threshing-machine and its operator, portrayed as resembling features of Hell, signigy the moral hell in which she now has to live.

Tess throughout the book is predominantly a victim, and there are a number of symbolic illustrations of her role. When she first leaves home to go to Trantridge, she is decked out in her best clothes by her mother. Mrs Durbeyfield is hopefully envisaging sexual conquest and resultant marriage for Tess, but her daughter is destined merely to be a victim of seduction, and the dressing-up therefore suggests ironically the preparation of a sacrificial victim. Another suggestion of a sacrifice is made when Tess, at the end of the book, lies down on an oblong slab at Stonehenge, like an animal about to be slain. The wounded pheasants which Tess sees during her tramping and in mercy kills symbolize her own deserted, abandoned, and mentally wounded state. And when she strikes Alec d'Urberville, at Flintcomb-Ash, with her heavy leather glove, the weapon she uses suggests a parallel with the mailed gauntlet of her d'Urberville forbears, but, ironically, only to point the contrast between the arrogant might of those bygone noble ancestors and the poverty and helplessness of their unfortunate little descendant.

Angel Clare, the man whom Tess loves, is predominantly a prig. This is not to say that he has not many good qualities also. He is genuinely sensitive and idealistic, and he often reveals his sensibility and thoughfulness during his courtship of Tess. It is little wonder that Tess, whose experience with d'Urberville has been so unhappy, almost worships the high-minded and fastidious Clare, and attributes to him perfect virtue and wisdom Unfortunately, Angel in reality is far less than what she thinks him. His studies have been desultory, and his modish liberal humanist opinions are largely untested; when shocked, as he is by Tess's disclosures, he immediately abandons his tolerant ideas, and retreats into the strictest conventional outlook. The reproaches which he throws at Tess could not be more conventional if he had been the most orthodox of church-goers: she must have been weak to let d'Urberville take advantage of her; she is now a different woman in his eyes; and they cannot live together in marriage for fear that they might have children who would reproach their parents with their mother's disgrace.

The reader can feel some sympathy for Angel Tess's confession is a great blow to an idealistic young Victorian man, especially when sprung on him on his wedding evening. But Angel is none the less repellent because of his hypocrisy; he confidently expects to have his own sexual escapade condoned; and, in his disillusionment, he sinks so low as to ask Izz, one of Tess's dairymaid friends, to go with him abroad as his mistress (although he quickly repents of this wild scheme).

Angel's chief defect is perhaps that he knows so little of life, as distinct from books and theories. He is humanized by his sufferings in Brazil (although one notices with distaste that he is more influenced towards tolerance by the opinions of a chance acquaintance than by the piteous pleas of his wife), and, in the end, he learns to accept Tess without judging her, even where her moral sense is so much in eclipse that she commits murder. 'Tenderness was absolutely dominant in Clare at last,' relates the narrative. Angel is saved as a man by his experiences, but at a terrible price—the destruction of the unfortunate Tess.

It is no accident that Hardy depicts Angel Clare, at the dairy, as playing a harp (very badly), while secluded in a garden which Tess, approaching to hear the loved young man's music, finds is full of poisonous weeds and insects. Angel's playing of the harp, together with his Christian name, suggest the outward appearance of exceptional goodness; but, when tested, he is to prove to be a greater poison in Tess's life than even the blatantly coarse d'Urberville.

Alec d'Urberville is in many ways the stock figure of the heartless, seducing squire. Some of his remarks might have been taken straight from some crude old melodrama. 'Ha-ha-ha! And what a crumby girl!' is his comment after his first meeting with Tess; much later he threatens her with: 'Remember, my lady, I was your master once. I will be your master again. If you are any man's wife you are mine!' His appearance, which includes 'an almost swarthy complexion', 'full lips', and a 'bold rolling eye', is equally that of the conventional villain. Hardy does not depict him as wholly bad (few people are); he has enough humanity to wish to help her and her family in their need. But he is always insensitive and self-seeking—Hardy sums him up as 'coarse'—and there is an insufferable complacency in his comments to Tess, whose life in Trantridge has been ruined by him: 'I suppose I am a bad fellow—a damn bad fellow. I was born bad, and I have lived bad, and I shall die bad in all probability.' Hardy symbolizes him as 'the blood-red ray' in the spectrum of Tess's life; d'Urberville, that is, stands for crude sex without love or tenderness.

The Durbeyfield parents, those perpetual blights on the life of Tess, are brilliantly portrayed in a few vivid sketches. John Durbeyfield is a lazy, feckless sot whose head, unluckily, is turned by the news of his noble ancestry. Optimistically, he hopes to be maintained by the antiquarians of the area because he is a relic of the nobility. Joan Durbeyfield, also lazy, careless, always behind with her household chores, is almost as bad, and is particularly culpable in that she lets her young daughter leave home without even preparing her to deal with unscrupulous admirers. Both parents, in their absurd hopes of benefits from their rich 'relatives', and their inability to fend for themselves, are a constant burden to the too-conscientious Tess.

Style

The style of this novel is, as always with Hardy, a mixture of good and bad. The dialogue gives many examples of this unevenness. Often, it is simple, direct, and moving: for example, in Tess's reproaches to her mother when she returns home from the d'Urberville household, or in her heart-broken pleas to Angel after her confession. The speech of the Durbeyfield parents is

pithy, vivid, and revealing. Joan Durbeyfield's comment when she
hears of Tess's seduction is, 'Well, we must make the best of it, I
suppose. 'Tis nater, after all, and what do please God!' remarks
which sum up very effectively her nature and attitude to life. On
the other hand, much of the speech of Angel Clare is stiff and
unnatural, as though to emphasize that Hardy is not good at
drawing an educated, idealistic young man of the middle class.
Here are two of his comments after Tess's confession:

'You were one person; now you are another. My God—how can
forgiveness meet such a grotesque—prestidigitation as that!'

and:

'You almost make me say you are an unapprehending peasant
woman, who have never been initiated into the proportion of
social things.'

It is difficult to believe that any man, even a prig like Clare,
could formulate such phrases in a moment of crisis.

The richness of the imagery has already been referred to. Note
particularly the passage, in Chapter XXV, in which Clare is
depicted as sensing the whole dairy permeated by the presence of
Tess. This extract reveals the imaginative sensibility of Angel, but
it also emphasizes the fact that his conception of her is idealistic
and visionary, and based on little understanding of her as a
person.

Some of the images introduced are connected with omens of
misfortune. For instance, a thorn from the roses that d'Urberville
gives Tess on her first visit to his home prick her chin—a sign of
ill-omen. On her wedding day, Tess momentarily sees her bridal
carriage as the old d'Urberville coach, a kind of hallucination
which is supposed to occur to members of her family when disaster
is imminent. That same wedding afternoon, a cock is heard to
crow in the dairy, a sound that, when heard at this time of the
day, apparently signifies either a bride's unchastity, or more
simply just ill-luck. Hardy, as an educated man, did not believe
these superstitions in the old sense, but he uses them skilfully to
build up a powerful atmosphere of fatality and impending
misfortune.

There is no true rustic chorus in this novel, but the ordinary
work people of Marlott, Trantridge, and Talbothays form part of

the background of the story. Most of them are characterized by kindliness and good nature. Their main defect is their crude insensitivity; to most of them, seduction is a joke. The dairymaids Izz and Marian, whose action contribute to the plot, and who are true friends to Tess, are given a measure of individuality.

Tess may be summed up as a brilliant novel, which shows with rare insight and sympathy how an inherently good person may be defeated largely through a combination of ill-luck and the selfishness of others. The book, which scandalized many sections of Victorian society when it appeared, did much to break down the prevailing convention that virginity was the sole attribute of importance in a woman, and its loss, regardless of circumstances, a profound disgrace.

7

Jude the Obscure

Following *Tess,* Hardy published in 1895 another novel which also
deeply shocked conventional public opinion, the attacks upon it
being indeed so bitter that Hardy gave up novel writing
altogether. This was *Jude the Obscure,* basically the story of a
studious working-class young man who wants to go to Oxford, and
is unable to do so for lack of means

Themes

Hardy himself, in his Preface to the first edition of the novel, has
set out what he considers to be the dominant themes of his own
work; the book according to him 'attempts to deal unaffectedly
with the fret and fever, derision and disaster, that may press in the
wake of the strongest passion known to humanity; to tell, without
a mincing of words, of a deadly war waged between flesh and
spirit; and to point the tragedy of unfulfilled aims.' The main
theme of the book is therefore one of inner conflict, the conflict
between a man's finer aims and aspirations and his more sensual
needs. It is the sexual weakness of the central character, Jude, who
is generally 'pushed around' by the women in his life, that
prevents the realization of his early ambitions.

The novel also raises the question of opportunities for gifted
working-class youth who, at the end of the nineteenth century,
had virtually none. Jude and Sue are two of the earliest
representatives in fiction of the talented proletariat, even though
they are notably isolated, and show virtually no solidarity with
their class as a whole. They are the only central characters in
Hardy's major novels, with the exception of Henchard, who may
be described as ambitious. While other Hardy heroes and
heroines, such as Tess, Winterborne, or Eustacia, aim at

happiness or goodness or both, Jude and Sue add to this wish their own high aspirations for education and achievement. It is mainly the conditions of their age which doom these aspirations to failure (even though the weaknesses of the pair also contribute to this), and there is everywhere in the book a strong criticism of the system that debars a studious youth like Jude from Oxford, while the idle sons of the well off are able to attend the university. This does not mean that Jude's academic aspirations, which may represent an over-estimation of his capacities, are not treated with considerable irony. The irony is there, but also the sympathy for a studious young man who is so conspicuously alone, without teachers, friends, counsellors of any kind. It would be a mistake, however, to see in Hardy a man so far in advance of his age that he is advocating general educational opportunities for the whole working class; social revolution of this magnitude would probably have been beyond his vision. Jude, who reads Latin and Greek as he drives his baker's van, is very obviously a special case, and his tragedy is that of the exceptional doomed to obscurity by a system that forbids him to entertain hopes not generally admitted to his class.

If the tragedy of Jude and Sue is primarily the tragedy of the aspiring in a world which puts only obstacles in their way, it is also the disaster of the non-conforming in a conventional world. The most obvious sign of their non-conformity is their unmarried state and the consequent illegitimacy of their children, but this in itself is merely one aspect of a general wish to be different, to be alone, not to form part of the community in which they find themselves. It is difficult to imagine *any* society, even one much more tolerant than the Victorian, into which Jude and Sue would fit easily, because they always judge issues from a personal and idiosyncratic, and not a social viewpoint. Society, which instinctively recognizes that they are different, hates and persecutes them for their non-conformity. One noticeable aspect of this, and one that removes any idea of this book being a working class manifesto, is that the persecution and ostracism are carried out as much by their fellow-members of the working class as by the classes in authority. It is the ordinary parishioners who object to their painting of the lettering of the church in Albrickham, and it is Jude's fellow-members of the Artisans'

Mutual Improvement Society who virtually force him to resign from the committee.

The novel also deals with important questions of sexual attraction and selection, marriage and divorce. Much of the scandal which the book aroused was due to the unusual honesty with which Hardy treated the theme of sexual selection. Jude is plainly shown as attracted to Arabella because she is 'a substantial female animal', and his feeling for her has neither real love nor respect; consequently, Hardy asserts that it is absurd that Jude and Arabella should enter into a lifelong contract on the basis of a brief, transitory impulse. Sue, equally, is shown as making a disastrous mistake in marrying Phillotson, and an even greater one in returning to him, since the truth is that she finds him sexually repulsive. Hardy's obvious belief — one which is generally accepted now, but was considered very daring at the time the novel was published — was that divorce should be easily obtainable where there was genuine incompatibility. He states his view in a later postscript to his Preface:

> My opinion at that time, if I remember rightly, was what it is now, that a marriage should be dissolvable as soon as it becomes a cruelty to either of the parties — being then essentially and morally no marriage . . .

Hardy, that is, bases the reality of marriage not on a legal contract or a formula recited in church, but on the genuine love and mutual regard of the partners.

The author also introduces the interesting idea that there may be certain persons and certain families unsuited to the formal ties of marriage. There is a kind of marital curse on Jude and Sue's family, the members of it having often contracted tragic unions. Sue, in particular, holds the theory that members of their family react against the formal union, and that they find happier partnerships when left legally free; it is largely because of this belief that she and Jude never marry. Possibly there is something morbid and neurotic in this distaste for the conventional union. After all, Jude and Sue's partnership is shown to be a good union, in the truest sense, if judged by Hardy's own standards, and their refusal to legalize what is virtually a genuine marriage subjects them to totally unnecessary censure and persecution. Still, Hardy is undoubtedly indicating that a marital union is one which should be freely chosen, and should not be an area where society dictates to individuals what they do.

The novel also paints a very unfavourable picture of the Christian Church, and specifically of the Established Church. The Church is depicted as out-of-date, unenlightened, a prop of the outmoded social system that, through its lack of educational opportunities and its insistence on permanent marriage, blights the happiness and aspirations of Jude and Sue. The fault of its clergy is that they act by the letter, in spite of the Biblical warning that 'the letter killeth'. In particular, the Christian concepts of self-sacrifice and submission are implicitly indicted through Sue's conversion to Christianity and her return, in a spirit of self-scourging, to her former husband, Phillotson. There is a bitter unconscious irony in the description given by Arabella of the congratulations extended to Jude by the officiating clergyman who re-marries Jude and Arabella, the irony being heightened by the fact that Jude has been made drunk by his bride in order to trap him into the ceremony. The union with Arabella is, as Jude himself declares, 'degrading, immoral, unnatural', and the clergyman, in praising it, is also merely going by the letter.

The novel obviously carries a number of important themes, and sometimes it is in danger if sinking beneath the weight of the various causes that Hardy is advocating in it. The time spent by Jude and Sue in discussing the issues of religion and marriage is considerable, and some parts of the novel read more like extracts from the report of a debating society than anything else. The book also suffers from the fact that it is not always clear whether the ills against which Hardy is crusading are remediable evils attributable to the social system, or are merely the necessary evils of the human condition. Certainly, progress since Hardy's own day has shown that the chief grievances which he illustrates, the lack of educational opportunities for the gifted working class and the permanence of the marriage tie in spite of incompatibility, are defects which can be remedied. But sometimes Hardy seems to be inveighing against less obviously remediable factors such as the institution of marriage itself, and here he is on less sure ground. Is not this the social order preferred by most people? If it were abolished, what would be put in its place? Admittedly, the marriage of Jude and Arabella is a great mistake, but it is an error freely entered into by the two persons concerned; it is hard to see how they could have been prevented from marrying if they wished to, and because of Arabella's deceitful and acquisitive nature, and Jude's gullibility and malleability, they *do* wish to marry.

The picture of Christminster (Hardy's fictional name for Oxford) given in the novel is an exceptionally original one. Numerous novels have depicted the town in its university aspect, from the viewpoint of dons or undergraduates. Hardy depicts it through the eyes of a working man, an outsider, and the Oxford which he shows is the town of slums and cheap lodging houses. No very flattering picture is painted of the university. Like so much else in the social system, it is out-moded, and neither its circumscribed, unsympathetic dons nor its idle, frivolous undergraduates are in any sense admirable

The contrast between the Christminster that Jude knows, and the Christminster which he aspires to know, but cannot, is very marked. Hardy, in a perceptive later comment, remarked that this was just one of many such contrasts in the novel. 'Of course,' he said, 'the book is all contrasts—or was meant to be in its original conception . . . e.g. Sue and her heathen gods set against Jude's reading the Greek Testament; Christminster academical, Christminster in the slums; Jude the saint, Jude the sinner; Sue the pagan, Sue the saint; marriage, no marriage; etc. etc.'

Assessment of plot

The book is characterized by a strong story. The central character, Jude, is a likeable and believable character, whose aspirations are made credible, and who is convincingly shown as defeated, partly by a combination of adverse circumstances, but also to a considerable extent by his own defects, which include weakness in dealing with women, excessive credulity, and a lack of practical common sense in making plans to try to further his aims.

The 'hour-glass' structure of the novel is very obvious; Jude, originally devout, gradually relinquishes his religious beliefs through his experiences of life, while Sue, initially sceptical, free-thinking, full of bright mockery, ends in a completely crushed submission to religious dogma. Perhaps there is too much a sense of obvious architecture in this. The contrasting developments of the pair are not entirely convincing. Jude's development to what is virtually a humanist position is probably the more believable part, made credible by the fact that first, his original position shows no very firm grasp of the central tenets of the Christian religion; secondly, the fact that in many ways he is natural man rather than spiritual man; and thirdly, that his shifting away from the Church is a slow and gradual development. The final conventional religiosity of Sue is less credible, mainly because it is so sudden a conversion. Hardy's explanation of it is that Sue is compelled into a complete *volte-face* by the tragedy of the deaths of her children, but, in order to make this convincing, he would have to depict Sue as characterized by very strong maternal feelings. This he nowhere does; Sue never carries conviction in the maternal role, and remains as bright, virginal, and as epicene a character when supposedly a mother as in the early part of the novel when Jude first meets her.

The central dramatic scene of the book, the murder of the children by little Father Time, is somewhat weak. The act, as carried out by a small boy, is too unnatural and bizarre to be easily believable. Hardy has done his best to make the strange tragedy convincing by depicting little Jude as a strange, melancholy, morbid child, old beyond his years, addicted to worrying about questions of lodgings and the burden that children represent to their elders. The attempt is not really successful; it is impossible to believe that so unnatural a small boy ever existed.

A few of the more minor aspects of the plot can be criticized. There are too many repetitive instances of Jude and Sue's half-heartedly making marriage plans and failing to carrying them out. There is little dramatic suspense here, because the perceptive reader will already have understood the pair's temperaments sufficiently well to realize that they will never contract a formal union. The occasional reappearances of Arabella in the story are too coincidental, and are often too obviously a means of advancing the plot. The only artistic reason why she re-enters the life of Jude at Aldbrickham is that Sue will become jealous of her and, in consequence, abandon her platonic relationship and allow Jude to become her lover.

Characters

The four main characters are very well drawn. There is a genuine mental and spiritual affinity between Jude and Sue — so great that even the unhappy Phillotson at first recognizes it. In their spirituality and unworldliness and very modern nervousness, they present a very obvious contrast to their more prosaic marriage partners, so that one scheme of characterization of the book could be regarded as Jude and Sue versus Arabella and Phillotson. Yet a degree of conflict is also apparent between Jude and Sue, mainly because Jude is a highly-sexed man with normal desires, and Sue is virtually sexless, granting Jude the physical relationship somewhat reluctantly as a concession. Because of this, some critics have tried to maintain that the true pattern of the book is Jude and Arabella versus Sue and Phillotson, Jude and Arabella being linked by sexual attraction, and Sue and Phillotson by their mutual coldness and unwillingness to give more than a part of themselves. Although an interesting theory, this seems to be easily disproved by the cat-and-dog life that Jude and Arabella lead, and by the even greater misery, the result of Sue's sense of physical repulsion, of the union between Sue and Phillotson. The true marriage, the union of hearts, exists between Jude and Sue in spite of their minor differences in temperaments.

Jude, the central character of the novel, is a believable and human character. He has very recognizable weaknesses, which make him endearing; he gets easily depressed (there is an early attempt at suicide), and he resorts to excessive drinking in moods of depression; he is soft with women, even with Arabella; he is credulous and easily fooled. These traits make him likeable, but one has to comment that they make it almost impossible for him to fulfil his ambitions; as a working-class man, Jude is faced by so many obstacles in the age in which he lives that he would need an exceptional degree of toughness, even of ruthlessness, to surmount them, and this he does not possess. His creator ironically depicts often just how ill qualified Jude is to fulfil his ambitions. The Christminster project is a dream — a lovely one admittedly, which Jude has little real hope of ever fulfilling. Naïvely, he imagines that living in Christminster near the academic world will help him to realize his aims, and it takes him some time to grasp the fact that residence there does not bring him into contact at all with the academic life which he covets. He appears to have no practical knowledge of the kind of training, such as that given in a Theological College or Training College, which might have been open to him. His theological ambitions, however, are almost laughable; his grasp of fundamental Christian teaching is so vague that the fact that he is, in furthering his relationship with Sue, disqualifying himself from the possibility of becoming a clergyman, takes a long time to strike him.

In many ways, Jude is very much a modern man: vague in his religious and humanitarian aspirations; rootless and alienated from the social life of the communities in which he lives; weak and confused in his relationships with women, whom he allows to push him around, but obviously very dependent on feminine company and support. His most attractive quality is that he does not become narrow or bitter in spite of the successive blows that life deals him; unlike Sue, he increases in breadth and broad-mindedness. Therefore, although the story of the frustration of his ambitions, culminating in his lonely death in lodgings in Oxford, is a deeply tragic one, it is not uniformly depressing; Jude shows throughout the book the resources of the human spirit when confronted by adversity.

Sue has been the subject of widely differing opinions from critics. To some, she is attractive because of a certain ethereal quality, together with her innocence of mind and bright intelligence; Jude pays her some of the loveliest tributes ever received by a woman in literature. An older critic writes of her: 'She is amazingly lovable. None of Hardy's most charming women . . . can compare with Sue for the strange and elusive delicacy of her charm.' But a modern critic has termed her the nastiest little bitch in English literature. This, no doubt, is because of her coquetry, her tendency to flirt and thereby arouse feelings that she has no intention of gratifying. Although always charming in manner, she is very selfish and inconsiderate in her treatment of the men in her life; the Christminster graduate who was her companion in what she insisted, despite his suffering, should remain a platonic relationship; Phillotson, whom she marries for her own convenience, although she does not love him; Jude, whom she also expects to remain a platonic friend after running away to him. At heart, she prefers companionship to passion, and resents men's demands on her. In many ways, Sue is obviously deeply neurotic, and one critic has perceptively pointed out that, in her neuroticism, she is showing remnants of the Victorianism that she is elsewhere rebelling against.

In other ways, Sue is very much the nineteenth-century emancipated woman, in her intellectualism and scepticism, and even in her overstrained nerves. (Her actions in running away from the Training College, and in running away from Phillotson by jumping out of the window are both impulsive actions that arise from pure nerves.) But one is not impressed by any sense of strength in her early intellectual agnostic position; she buys statuettes of Pagan deities in preference to those of the saints, but has not the nerve to tell her employer what they represent. This tendency to give in perhaps forecasts her final submission to conventional religion.

Phillotson is in many ways a lesser Jude. The tragedy of his unfulfilled ambitions is as stark as Jude's, and he has not even any private happiness to compensate for this failure. Initially, he impresses by his liberal qualities and sense of justice; he shows exceptional generosity, for the Victorian age, in letting Sue go to Jude. Unfortunately, the poverty and ostracism that he encounters because of his humane behaviour cause him to lose all his earlier tolerance; he ends sadly in a 'reactionary spirit', resolved on 'judicious severity' with the returned Sue, and becomes nearer in outlook to his friend Gillingham, who stands for average public opinion. Phillotson's chief misfortune is that he is unattractive to women; Sue is not alone in finding him repulsive as a man, as the frank comments of her great-aunt Drusilla make perfectly clear.

Arabella is depicted as high-spirited, sensual, and selfish. Her appeal is to the more basic passions; she cannot understand any of the finer and more spiritual aspects of life; Jude's love for Sue and his Christminster aspirations are alike incomprehensible to her, and excite only her jealousy. Significantly, many even of her obvious charms, such as her hair or her dimples, are wholly or partly false. Arabella gets by very adequately in life—much better than either Jude or Sue—because she has no scruples. She tricks Jude twice into marriage, does not jib at bigamy, and is encouraging a new admirer, the quack Vilbert, while Jude lies dead in his lodgings. Her attitude to men and marriage is one of cynical opportunism, as his advice to Sue on the topic makes clear. Her temporary religious conversion is as unconvincing as that of Alec d'Urberville, and like him, she soon abandons her new faith when she meets again the sexually desired object, flinging her tracts into the hedge when she encounters Jude again. Undeniably, she is something of a card, and there is much humour in the treatment of her. Jude in the end regards her as a source of amusement, the best or perhaps only way to treat her.

Some of the novel, for example the endless discussions of Jude and Sue on the marriage theme, shows a fatigued invention, but much of it is distinguished by a genuine artistry. The wish of the youthful Jude to go to Oxford is made intelligible by the boy's vision of the 'city of light' on the horizon, and by the man's conjuring up the images of the distinguished men who once studied there. The novel is suffused with irony; for example, the dreamy Jude, newly arrived at Christminster, wanders round the colleges, fingering their carvings, only to be moved on by a policeman who suspects him of being an undesirable vagrant. There is an obvious ironic contrast between the studious Jude, who cannot enter the university, and the idle undergraduates who are chiefly interested in sporting pups and boat races.

Sometimes, Hardy's bitter irony is too laboured and obvious. For example, the reader can see for himself what a travesty of marriage the union of Jude and Arabella is, without needing Hardy's heavy comments on the ceremony. Similarly, the irony of two clergymen discussing the eastward position when Sue and Jude are in anguish over the deaths of their children is obvious enough, without Jude's bitter comment: 'They are two clergymen of different views, arguing about the eastward position. Good God—the eastward position, and all creation groaning!'

The narrative is well-constructed, with a skilful linking of earlier and later episodes. It begins with a parting—that of Phillotson for Oxford—a fitting opening for a novel that is full of partings and journeys. Both Phillotson and the quack doctor Vilbert, introduced early in the story, are cleverly worked in to the later development. The portrait of the boy Jude is excellent, because it shows in him the qualities which will develop to the full

in the grown man: the love of books, the tenderness to all living
creatures, the depression, and the wish not to grow up.

Style

Jude the Obscure is a less obviously poetically integrated book
than *Tess*; the predominantly urban settings do not lend
themselves so obviously to the use of imagery. Still, there are a few
memorable images; for example, the flowers at the agricultural
show and little Father Time's comment on them: 'I should like the
flowers very very much, if I didn't keep on thinking they'd all be
withered in a very few days!' This symbolizes the transitory nature
of all life and beauty, and ironically presages the boy's later killing
of himself, and of Jude and Sue's two children. The symbolism
here is often criticized as too obvious, but it at least emphasizes the
morbid, negative outlook of the small boy.

The symbolism associated with Arabella is significant; the
images connected with her are predominantly those of pigs and
the pig industry, and of drink and bars, emphasizing Arabella's
gross and sensual nature. The cochin's egg which she hatches in
her bosom stands for her unthinking acceptance of the Life Force,
while the love filter which Vilbert gives her stresses the importance
she attaches to blind sexual attraction. Conversely, Sue is
associated with the image of the pigeons which she rescues from
the poulterers and sets free, symbolizing possibly the wish of Sue's
spiritual nature to be free from earthly restraints. The rabbit
caught in a trap, which is mercifully killed by Jude, may also
possibly symbolize Sue, caught like a defenceless creature (even
though it is by her own initiative) in the snare of an unhappy
marriage.

There is no true rustic chorus in this novel of predominantly
urban settings. The nearest approximation to it is Widow Edlin,
the old nurse of great-aunt Drusilla and friend of Jude and Sue.
Her pithy comments on their failure to carry out their marriage
plan, and on Sue's action in returning to the hated Phillotson,
represent a chorus of earthy common sense on the exalted
absurdities of the younger people.

Jude the Obscure may be summed up as a novel of great power,
if also sometimes revealing a fatigued invention which shows itself
in too much repetitive action and debate-like dialogue. It

sometimes threatens to be a failure through the very multiplicity of the causes that Hardy is championing, but succeeds in spite of this, through its imaginative realization of conflict and aspiration embodied in the characters of Jude and Sue.

Hardy's last novel to be published (although it was not the last written) is *The Well-Beloved* (1897), which deals with the idealizing love of a sculptor, Pierston, for three women of successive generation of the same family. It is probably the most absurd of all Hardy's works. The initial idea, that of depicting the romantic, idealizing artistic temperament, and the difficulties into which it leads its possessor, is interesting, but the treatment of the theme, involving as it does the failure of Pierston to know intimately any of the women whom he admires, is too negative to give the book any significance.

8

Hardy In His Times

Hardy, like most gifted artists, was in many ways very much a man of his age, although in others conspicuously in advance of it. This is not to say that the social conditions of the era in which he lived were a primary stimulus to his creative activity; but merely that he was sensitive to them, and that this awareness appears in his work.

Agricultural and industrial reform

Hardy lived in an age of transition and great social upheaval. England was slowly developing from its former state of a mainly agricultural country to its new condition of a primarily industrial society. The old settled agricultural order was breaking up; many of the cottagers who held their small houses as copyholders or leaseholders were being deprived of their homes as their leases expired, and in consequence were forced to move into the expanding towns for work. The country environment itself was subject to change, chiefly by the introduction of new machinery which threatened to reduce the farm worker to a mere operative. Another innovation which brought about observable changes was the railway, whose introduction into ever-widening areas greatly increased the mobility of the country-dweller. (The number of train journeys featuring in Hardy's novels is quite high, and sometimes, as in *Jude* and *A Pair of Blue Eyes*, these contribute significantly to the plot.)

The reflections of these changes are seen very clearly in the novels of Hardy. Sometimes, as in *The Woodlanders* or *Tess,* the loss of cottagers' homes to the landowner is significant to the plot; in one novel, *Jude the Obscure,* the country-born central character is shown as forsaking rural life entirely for the world of the town. More importantly, Hardy often depicts the whole rural environment as subject to transition, invaded by aliens and innovators, with a very limited power to resist the intruders (notably in *Under the Greenwood Tree, The Woodlanders, Tess*). This is not to say that Hardy necessarily regretted the changes; he may well have thought some of them beneficial or unavoidable. As a countryman by birth, but also an educated professional man who had lived in London, Hardy had an ambivalent attitude towards rural life. In his novels, he celebrates its richness, and in particular that of its old culture and customs, but at the same time he recognizes its stagnation and frequent need of revitalizing forces (particularly in *Far From the Madding Crowd* and *The Return of the Native*). Certainly, he appears to have little doubt that modernity will triumph. Farfrae, in *The Mayor of Casterbridge*, is the victor over Henchard at least partly because, unlike his rival, he is a man disposed to welcome new ideas. In *A Laodicean*, a potentially interesting novel which develops disappointingly, the new owner of the old aristocratic castle is a modern heroine who has inherited the wealth created by her father, an industrial pioneer.

Breakdown of the classes

This upheaval was accompanied by a general social break-up which caused many gifted men, including Hardy, to question the validity of the old social order which hitherto had prevailed largely unquestioned. Until the late Victorian Age, the classes had been firmly established in their determined places, with some degree of social mobility both upwards and downwards, but generally a clear gap between the gentry and upper middle and professional classes and the lower working classes. This had been accepted unquestioningly by novelists such as Jane Austen or Trollope, and lesser popular fiction had often stressed, not merely the greater prosperity and refinement of the upper classes, but also their greater natural superiority and worth.

By the latter half of the Victorian Age, such easy assumptions were increasingly challenged by writers and thinkers. Hardy's own somewhat uncertain social origin, in a class somewhere between the professional classes and the cottagers, together with his own professional training, made him acutely aware of class distinctions, and of the injustices suffered by the lower classes, and his personal experience of fashionable society, in which he never felt greatly at ease, made him critical of the more cultivated classes. Consequently, in defiance of much prevailing tradition, it is the poor and humble whom he makes his heroes and heroines. He is an innovator in that he depicts the frequently uneducated poor as, not merely as good as, but intrinsically better than their social superiors. The lower classes in his books are shown as possessing greater humanity, kindness, and truthfulness than those in a higher social position. His portraits of the wealthy or cultivated are usually critical and satirical, the examples of Mrs Charmond, Fitzpiers, Miss Aldclyffe, d'Urberville, Wildeve, and the fashionable people in *The Hand of Ethelberta* being outstanding. Hardy proclaims the worth of the intelligent proletariat in his portraits of Jude and Sue, Tess and Giles Winterborne, and in this he is a man in advance of his age. At the same time, he has no illusions about the handicaps from which they suffer; the poverty and resultant insecurity of these characters are obvious, and do much to destroy their happiness.

Two of the buttresses of the old social order were the aristocracy and the Established Church. Hardy clearly regarded both as outmoded institutions which had outlived their usefulness, and his portrayals of both are hostile and satirical. Snobbery is shown as unjustifiable on the part of a useless and corrupt upper class, and the portrait of Lord Mountclere, the randy, ludicrous old nobleman in *The Hand of Ethelberta,* in itself an attack on the entire peerage, may be regarded as an indictment of a system which exacts on behalf of such men deference and respect from their fellows.

Similarly, the Established Church is represented by Hardy as narrow, lifeless, out of touch with people and with the times; this is especially true of *Jude the Obscure*, in which the Church stands for all the repressive forces which thwart Jude and Sue. Individual clergy in Hardy's novels are often portrayed as good and well-meaning, if unremarkable men (although there is also a fair sprinkling of the snobbish and the worldly); the village parson in *Tess* and Mr Torkingham in *Two on a Tower* are both estimable men, although Hardy, typically, depicts them as largely ineffectual, unable to do or say much to help those in their care. In spite of his unbelief, Hardy always remained something of a 'churchy' man, who wished that he could accept church dogmas, and might fairly be termed a wistful agnostic. He remained conscious of the Church as an institution in the life of the community—as indeed, any Victorian who had been devout in youth could scarcely fail to do—and the novels give church services and the clergy a fair amount of prominence.

Victorian philosophers

Hardy's opposition to the Church was a fundamental one; he was unable to accept the supernatural and redemptive doctrines which are the foundations of Christianity. His gradual development to the scepticism which marked many Victorian thinkers owed much to his studies of the great rationalist philosophers and scientists of the age. Hardy had read, probably before he first left Dorset, Darwin's famous work, *Origin of Species,* which must have drastically undermined his already uncertain religious beliefs. This revolutionary work, by showing that the universe was the result of evolutionary processes, seemed to many to exclude any possibility of its being the subject of supernatural care. Darwin indicated that, in his view, there was no evidence of beneficent design in the ordering of the world, and ample proof of the cruelty and pain in nature resulting from the struggle for survival.

To this path-breaking work, Hardy added the reading of other powerful Victorian sceptics: Spencer, Huxley, John Stuart Mill. The contributions of these men to current thinking all had their distinctive elements, but all shared a scientific or naturalistic view of the world which excluded a religious explanation of its development, together with a belief in the impersonal and unmoral nature of whatever unknown underlies scientific phenomena. The world, according to them, is not primarily benevolent, but uncaring; man is not a godlike being, the subject of Divine favour, but an evolved creature who is mainly the product of his environment, and whose destiny is largely determined by impersonal forces over which he has no control, his only distinguishing characteristics being his limited free will and his power of rational thinking.

This somewhat grim creed can be seen expressed in all Hardy's major novels. His characters are depicted as having their destinies virtually determined by fate and by environment. Contrary to what is sometimes alleged, Hardy's individuals do have a measure of free will, an area in which they can make choices, but it has to be admitted that this free will is shown as very limited in scope. The characters could be summed up as having an obvious choice to act well or badly in the circumstances in which they find themselves, but little hope of changing the circumstances radically, or of moving completely out of an unfavourable environment. They are primarily subject to chance and fate, which are indiscriminate in their effects. It follows that, in Hardy's novels, fate can bring good fortune as well as bad, as the eventual destinies of Gabriel Oak and Elizabeth-Jane Henchard show; but the author's own pessimistic cast of thought ensures that chance, for his characters, is much more often adverse than benevolent.

In his tragic vision of life, Hardy is very much at variance with the prevailing tone of most of the Victorian thinkers who influenced him. Most of these were characterized by a robust optimism. Although stressing that the universe was unmoral, and man's fate largely determined by neutral impersonal forces, they had great hopes of what he could achieve because of his distinctive attribute, his rational mind; they believed that evolution and a greater use of reason were gradually leading to a saner and juster universe. Hardy shared some of their optimism about social progress; his championing of social causes expressed in *Tess* and *Jude* indicates that he considered that some social evils were remediable, and both books had in fact some influence in changing public opinion.

Hardy's cast of mind, however, was profoundly different from that of the philosophers whose teachings he followed; his thinking was less rigorous and logical than theirs, but, as an artist, he was characterized by greater sensibility and deeper emotional reactions to the world. Consequently, the pain and suffering in the universe, which the philosophers accepted equably as an observable fact, caused great anguish to Hardy's deeply sensitive nature; the world, he felt bitterly, ought to be a better place than it was. And whereas many of the sceptical thinkers either dismissed the loss of religious belief as a welcome emancipation from irrational superstition, or else found that they had never had any belief to begin with, Hardy, like many sensitive Victorians who had been brought up in the tradition faith, suffered profound distress at being obliged, intellectually, to repudiate religion. A distinctive feature of his novels — perhaps their most outstanding feature — is the sense of the suffering of the world that permeates them, coupled with a degree of resentment at the unmoral nature of the universe and the apparent absence of a benevolent deity.

The woman question

Another social question which was coming into prominence in the Victorian Age, and of which Hardy's novels indicate some awareness on the part of the author, was the position of women. A new type of woman, confident of the value of her opinions, forthright in expression, independent because she lived by her own paid employment, was making her presence felt, and Hardy, in his portrait of Sue Bridehead, has given a very vivid depiction of this emancipated type. However, in showing Sue as a creature largely governed by nerves, and in bringing her, at the end of *Jude,* to intellectual and moral collapse, involving the repudiation of her earlier liberal views, Hardy is revealing considerable pessimism about woman's ability to sustain an independent role throughout life. His comments on the weaker sex in his description of the young girl students at Sue's Training College shows that he considered woman's inferiority innate, and therefore scarcely capable of being overcome either by determination or by education. At heart, he held the Victorian man's belief that a woman needed a man for support, and certainly, he makes love the most important experience in the lives of all his heroines. Still, he also seems to offer the tentative opinion that women might accomplish more, and avoid their worst errors, if their education gave them a better training for the realities of life. The fault of Grace Melbury's fashionable schooling is that it fits her for little but decorative gentility, and consequently obliges her to grasp at the first eligible suitor. The upbringing of Bathsheba is inadequate because it gives her no training in managing the farm of which she is heiress.

This listing of the social questions of the day shows that Hardy himself was often aware of important contemporary public issues. But it is noticeable that his heroes and heroines, although sometimes conscious of these issues themselves, nowhere show any strong inclination to join the communal movements that can alter unsatisfactory social conditions. They are all individualists, too engrossed in their own private affairs, and perhaps also too diffident, to play a leading role in any club or society formed with the intention of pressing for changes in the existing laws. A more forceful heroine than Grace Melbury would have *campaigned* for a change in the divorce laws, instead of meekly allowing them to destroy her happiness. A Jude with more of the qualities of leadership would have used his intellectual gifts, as other working-class champions of the time did, to agitate for educational opportunities for the gifted young people of his class. Hardy's characters, although sometimes outspoken in private conversation or in isolated incidents, tend normally to submit to the status quo, and many of them, such as Henchard, Jude, and Tess, are scarcely integrated at all with society.

In a world in which social order is being disrupted and religion has to a great extent lost its sanctions, the emphasis is on the private concerns of the individual, and especially on his sexual life. Love assumes an outstanding importance in the lives of characters when they have no very strong loyalties to religious or political creeds; and one critic has perceptively remarked that, in Hardy's novels, love is the crucial ground on which men and women stake everything. Hardy's individuals expect a great deal from love, as indeed they do from life in general and, inevitably, they are frequently disappointed. Bathsheba, Boldwood, Eustacia and Clym, Winterborne, Tess make of the object of their affections an ideal which does not correspond with reality, and disillusionment is the natural outcome. Often, in Hardy's world, love is not returned, at least not to the same degree as it is given, and the characters no doubt value the person they cannot have all the more because he is unattainable. In the novels, there is an observable marked stress on infidelity and betrayal; happy marriages are rare. Therefore, although love plays such a prominent role in the lives of Hardy's characters, it is rarely an experience that increases their happiness. Too much, indeed, is staked by them on love, and their choices are often disastrous because, too often, the judgement and prudence of the characters are overthrown by the force of their emotions.

Hero or anti-hero

This excessive emphasis on sexual love, and especially on the validity of the feeling as a basis for marital choice, is a very modern phenomenon. Very modern, too, is the kind of hero whom Hardy often creates. He is primarily the "anti-hero," the man who is at the mercy of life, and, though sometimes capable of aspiration and thought, is not strong enough to carve out his destiny in the way he wishes. Frequently, he is something of a dreamer, tossed about by life, and also pushed about, or at least overshadowed, by the woman in his life. Jude, Clym, Winterborne, Fitzpiers, Wildeve, and, to some extent, Knight and Angel Clare, all bear the marks of this type. Often there is descernible in Hardy's men—and to some degree in his women, too—a modern malaise, a vague discontent, and a yearning for some person or set of circumstances beyond their reach. Sometimes, the sense of disenchantment with life as it is is so great that the individual expresses a desire not to live at all, as Jude, Tess, Clym, and Henchard all illustrate at some point in their lives; and, in a few instances, as with Henchard, Elfride, and possibly Giles Winterborne, the character dies because circumstances have been so adverse that he no longer feels any wish to live.

What the modern reader perhaps finds most rewarding in Hardy's fiction, apart from the poetic integration of thought and language, is the psychological insight into character which he reveals. While other Victorian novelists chronicled mainly observable surface behaviour, Hardy is primarily interested in mental states which cause his characters to act as they do. Instead of castigating evil or weakness, he traces it to its causes, and leads the reader to understand rather than to censure. He portrays Henchard as motivated by a blind urge towards self-destruction, Jude as ruined by his dependence on women, Tess as led to disaster by a certain yielding quality in her attitude to sexual relations. He understands that misconduct is more often the product of weakness than of evil, and points to the restlessness and rootlessness which are the causes of the sexual infidelity of Fitzpiers, Wildeve, and Eustacia. In an age which liked the good and the bad to be clearly distinguished, Hardy is uniquely adult in recognizing that, in real life, there are few real heroes and few real villains; most people are a believable mixture of both, probably more often well-intentioned and weak than deliberately malevolent. Here, he is in advance of the general level of thinking of his day, and looks forward to the greater psychological understanding of the twentieth century.

Hardy as innovator

Writing as he did at the close of the nineteenth century, Hardy in his art often shows traces of both nineteenth and twentieth-century features of the novel. The tradition in which he began writing was that of a placid, conventional, and painstaking realism, and he often shows the continued influence of this tradition, especially in *The Woodlanders* and *The Mayor of Casterbridge*. But more often, Hardy is consciously breaking away from the older tradition, and struggling independently towards a new symbolized style of fiction. This is shown by the unusual nature of some of the characters whom he creates, and by his deep psychological comprehension of their emotions and their thinking; by the unexpected and sometimes fantastic nature of the incidents he uses in his plots; and above all by his use of symbols and images to convey meaning. Here Hardy is an innovator, consciously rejecting an outmoded convention, and looking forward to the developments in fiction of Joseph Conrad and André Gide.

This chapter has recounted something of the social conditions of Hardy's day, which are mirrored in his work. It should, however, be emphasized that Hardy raises public issues in only a very fragmentary and desultory fashion, and then only as primarily in their effects on the private lives of individuals. The reader who regards Hardy's novels mainly as illustrations of the social background of the age (as historians are sometimes inclined to do), is in danger of missing the most valuable part of what Hardy has to offer: a deeply prophetic tragic vision of life, and a creative and imaginative depiction of the lives and developments of individual characters. Similarly, while it is helpful to show how Hardy's achievement is related to the movements in literature which preceded and succeeded his work, such an analysis would be a hindrance rather than a help if it obscured the deeply personal nature of the vision and mind of the author.

9

The Strength and Weaknesses of Hardy's Technique

The weaknesses of Hardy as a writer are very obvious, and there is considerable agreement among critics about the chief defects in his art. He is a novelist whom it is easy to belittle or patronize, if the critic so wishes, because the faults in his writing are glaring and can readily be illustrated by quotation. It is a grave mistake, however, to underestimate Hardy. He has won the high place which he holds in English literature because, if his weaknesses are substantial, his strengths are colossal, and are the marks of a great man who possessed a serious and thoughtful mind and a true creative vitality.

In many ways, Hardy's virtues and defects are inseparable. A familiar (and quite justified) criticism of his major novels is the restricted nature of their range, yet it is no doubt this very limitation which accounts for the fidelity with which he depicts the rather circumscribed area which he has selected. He avoids dealing with public, intellectual, and social life in his best work, and he is notoriously bad at portraying public events of fashionable life. (To quote one critic, Hardy could no more describe a sophisticated party than Meredith a Wessex milking.) Instead, he deliberately elects to depict a restricted, obscure, often backward rural world, 'the cool sequestered vale of life', in which the lives of the chief characters are remote from the busy world of public issues and 'ignoble strife', and their 'sober wishes' are centred on humdrum work, their families, and their private predicaments and emotions. It is because of this deliberate concentration, in addition to his own intimate knowledge, that Hardy is able to portray the area of life which he has chosen with such sureness of touch. In his major works, he writes well within his own range. And the exclusion of public issues is amply compensated for by the vitality and imagination with which Hardy depicts the private concerns of individuals.

Again, the criticism can be levelled at Hardy that he is incapable of sustaining high comedy throughout a novel, as *The Hand of Ethelberta* shows, or of writing a work of consistent satirical irony, as the limited achievement of *A Pair of Blue Eyes* makes clear. But this is merely to say that Hardy, is spite of the humour with which he often portrays his rustics, is primarily a serious writer whose best works are deeply serious, and whose mind is incapable of frivolity for long.

Character

Allied to the restricted range of Hardy's themes are the obvious limits to his power of delineating character. He is generally unimpressive in depicting the upper classes and fashionable people. His cultivated ladies, such as Mrs Charmond, Lucetta, and Paula Power, are mainly stereotyped stock figures. His well-to-do villains, for example d'Urberville and, to some extent Fitzpiers, are conventional evil-doers. His serious intellectual professional men such as Angel Clare, Knight, and George Somerset emerge merely as unlikeable prigs.

In the major novels, such failures are atoned for by Hardy's more successful character studies. The main reason for the limited achievement of the minor novels is that Hardy, in these, is dealing mainly with upper and professional class life, of which he has limited knowledge, and with whose values, prejudices, and failings he has virtually no sympathy. He shows very limited skill in delineating characters who move in these circles, and there is an observable falsity and artificiality in his studies of the cultivated classes.

It is a commonplace of criticism to say that Hardy's true talent in characterization is shown in his depiction of the rural poor, whom he understands and with whom he sympathizes. However, it is very noticeable that Hardy selects for his main characters men and women, who, though identified in their poverty and obscurity with their fellows, are to a considerable extent distinguished from them by greater nobility of character, and fineness of feeling. Materially, they are submerged in the mass; morally, they rise above it. In Oak, Winterborne, Tess and Marty, for example, Hardy portrays characters whose essential purity of spirit shines out in the monotonous obscurity of lives dominated by hard work and poverty. Their innate nobility survives the most adverse of circumstances. Indeed, one criticism of them that might be made is that, given their restricted background and the commonness of most of their families and neighbours, their nobility almost passes belief. The sustained loyal devotion of Oak, the generous self-sacrifice of Winterborne, and the fine moral scruples of Tess seem almost unbelievable in characters who might be expected to be made more narrow by a pinched, poverty-stricken way of life. All that can be said is that Hardy's belief is that there exists a supreme natural goodness which owes nothing to cultivation, education, or even example, and that the reader must enter into Hardy's conviction regarding this possibility.

It is noticeable that Hardy's women characters are often more interesting than the men. Like many artists, Hardy had a strong feminine strain in his nature, which gave him an ability to understand the emotional reactions of women. It is probable, too, that the naturally weaker postion of women in the world also inspired in him a sympathy for their situation.

Fate

It has often been remarked that there is a distinct stress in Hardy's novels on accident and unlikely coincidence; most of his plots ninge on the chance workings of fate. Here, however, a distinction must be drawn between the minor and the major works. In the minor novels, the emphasis is on the events caused by a purely external chance; the arbitrary nature of these happenings makes them unconvincing, as also does their excessive number; one critic counted no less than forty chance accidents of fate in *A Pair of Blue Eyes*. By contrast, while the major novels admittedly all contain some unlikely episodes, which have been referred to in the analysis of individual novels, it is noteworthy that their most important incidents give the effect of an emotional truth, because they accord both with what we know of the characters and with the action that has preceded them. The scene in which Bathsheba opens Fanny's coffin, the flight and death of Eustacia and Wildeve, the evasions of Tess to Angel Clare, the burning of his theological books by Jude as an indication that he relinquishes his hopes of being a clergyman, are all incidents which carry conviction, because the reader is persusaded that, the characters being as they are, this is a possible and even likely way for them to behave. Certainly, the stress in Hardy does seem to be on the malign nature of Fate, but this must be accepted as inseparable from the author's whole vision of life. It is not correct to say that chance in Hardy's novels is *always* adverse, though it often is; one can cite instances, such as Henchard drawing back from suicide because he sees his own effigy in the river, or Grace and Fitzpiers escaping unharmed from the man-trap laid for Fitzpiers, where it must be admitted that chance is working for the characters. Nor is it correct to say that Hardy's characters are manipulated by fate, so that they have no reasonable possibility of averting disaster. They always have the possibility of acting other than they do, although the area in which their free will operates is always depicted as limited. Tess could not, perhaps, effect an immediate reconciliation with Clare once he leaves her, and still less could she obliterate the memory of her past seduction; but she does have the possibility of persevering in her plan to see Clare's parents, and thus possibly be eventually re-united with him. In Hardy's best novels, it is the characters themselves who are ultimately responsible for their own destinies; character, indeed, is fate.

In addition, some of the stranger episodes in Hardy's major novels must be viewed as a deliberate venturing by the author from the dull world of prosaic realism into the realm of the fantastic. Examples are the wife-sale in *The Mayor of Casterbridge,* Eustacia's dressing-up as a boy mummer in *The Return of the Native,* and Troy's appearance as Dick Turpin in a travelling fair in *Far From the Madding Crowd.* Hardy is here consciously trying to use fantasy creatively, and the incidents must be regarded as deliberate artistic attempts to avoid dullness. The criterion of whether they are acceptable or not should not be their inherent strangeness (for they are all very odd incidents), but whether, as described, they carry an artistic conviction. The first two of these three incidents listed seem to me to be on the whole successful; in the wife-sale, the development of Henchard's action through the gradual building up of drunken bad temper makes his bizarre auction finally believable; while Eustacia's boredom, recklessness, disregard of conventions, and curiosity to see Clym, combine to make it credible that she should masquerade as one of the mummers. The play-acting of Troy is less believable, since it is hard to credit either that a lover of good-living, such as he is, should consent to live in such poverty and insecurity while he has a wealthy wife at home, or that he should risk playing such a humiliating role so near to Weatherbury. Significantly, these two considerations later cause him to give up his temporary role, and return home to claim his wife.

Melodrama

These deliberate attempts at an effective use of fantasy must be distinguished from the frequent artificial and melodramatic situations which can be found in abundance in the minor novels. A favourite device of Hardy's is to use a situation in which a number of persons, unaware of each other's presence, are acting in an identical place. For example, one of the most melodramatic scenes in *Desperate Remedies* is that in which the villain buries the body of his wife by night, watched, unknown to himself, by three different people. A central scene in *The Hand of Ethelberta* is that in which Ethelberta is pursued at Rouen by three suitors, none of whom is aware of the others' presence. Such devices are ingenious, but no more, and the reader is always conscious of their artificiality and of the obvious fact that they are mere clever substitutes for the more genuinely conceived creative action found in the major works.

An interesting aspect of Hardy's use of the fantastic is his frequent introduction of an element of the supernatural. Examples are the burning by Susan Nonsuch, in *The Return of the Native,* of a wax model of Eustacia, who is soon to die tragically; or Henchard's secret visit to a conjuror to consult him about the likelihood of a good harvest. Hardy is here deliberately using the old beliefs to build up atmosphere, and induce a sense of fatality. He himself did not fully believe in such superstitions, in the old sense, but he knew that they were part of the folk-lore of the country, and that many people still retain a half-belief in their validity (as the popularity of horoscopes and palmistry even yet makes clear). He skilfully uses the average person's sense of the mystery of fortune and fatality to heighten the impression of the strangeness of life and of fate which his plots emphasize.

Style

Hardy's style has been, understandably enough, the subject of harsh criticism. One modern critic, asserting in a pained fashion that 'the style seems almost wholly bad', upbraids him for the use of heavy, ponderous words, and a failure to write simply and straightforwardly. This is so often true that only a fervent, uncritical admirer of Hardy could deny it. Yet a good deal can be said on the other side, too. One point about Hardy's novels is that he sometimes writes simply and directly, especially in his more dramatic scenes, so that it is unfair to select his most involved passages, and leave the impression that Hardy is always guilty of the use of cumbersome words and awkward circumlocutions. Another point is that the sheer creative vitality of his best works often carries the reader across the worst paragraphs. The whole of a chapter in one of the major novels often leaves a powerful impression even where individual passages can be seriously criticized on stylistic grounds. Hardy is not a writer to be read in small sections with a hypersensitive regard to the precise expression of individual paragraphs, but an author with whom it is preferable to read a number of chapters at a sitting in order to appreciate the flow and vitality of the narrative.

It may also be added that even cumbersome passages in Hardy have their compensating virtues. Take, for instance, the following extract from *Tess*, in which Angel Clare muses on the reflections that Tess makes on life to him.

He was surprised to find this young woman — who though but a milk-maid had just that touch of rarity about her which might make her the envied of her housemates — shaping such sad imaginings. She was expressing in her own native phrases — assisted a little by her Sixth Standard training — feelings which might almost have been called those of the age — the ache of modernism. The perception arrested him less when he reflected that what are called advanced ideas are really in great part but the latest fashion in definition — a more accurate expression, by words in *logy* and *ism,* of sensations which men and women have vaguely grasped for centuries. (Chapter XIX)

This, though by no means the worst example which could be produced from Hardy, does illustrate some of his typical faults; one notices the involved, awkwardly constructed sentences, with frequent parentheses; and the heavy phrases such as 'the perception arrested him less . . .' or 'a more accurate expression, by words in *logy* and *ism,* of sensations . . .' Yet what strikes one also is the richness of ideas apparent in the extract. In one brief paragraph, Hardy has introduced concepts which could lead the thoughtful reader to reflect for a long time on the implications of this single paragraph. Hardy undoubtedly often writes clumsily, but he writes creatively, and he does so because, pre-eminently, he has something to say; at times, one has the impression that his mind is so fertile in ideas that he must struggle to express them, and his style bears the mark of that struggle. A faultless and elegant style is only too often the gift of a writer who has a limited stock of ideas to express.

Hardy possibly suffers in present-day estimation from the fact that in the past it was often his more pretentious pieces of writing that impressed critics most; these leave the modern reader cold. The description of Egdon Heath, in the first chapter of *The Return of the Native,* was formerly much admired, but is now generally considered to be marred by theatricality. Another extract which won great popularity was the scene in *A Pair of Blue Eyes* in which Knight, who has fallen over a cliff, and is clinging to its side in peril of his life, muses on the geological history of the world. The Victorians were impressed by the nature of Knight's philosophizing, whereas a modern reader is merely conscious of how unlikely it is that he should be indulging in such calm meditation at a moment of supreme danger. Conversely, the modern is often interested in those aspects of Hardy that made the Victorians most uneasy; in particular the descriptions of character that reveal a deep psychological insight. Hardy is strangely modern himself here, whether he is describing the weakness of Jude, the self-destructiveness of Henchard, or the restlessness and the lack of seriousness that make philanderers of Troy, Wildeve, and Fitzpiers.

Author's interference

One fault of Hardy's which is particularly obtrusive is his practice of intruding his personal comments on events into the narrative. Often these comments slow the story in an irritating way, and frequently they underline the tragedy or irony of incidents in a heavy fashion, when the reader hardly needs to have the significance of the preceding action pointed out to him. Sometimes, too, the comment is singularly inappropriate to what has gone before. Consider, for instance, this bitter passage containing Clym's reflections on the tragic drowning of Eustacia and Wildeve towards the end of *The Return of the Native:*

> He did sometimes think he has been ill-used by fortune, so far as to say that to be born is a palpable dilemma, and that instead of men aiming to advance in life with glory they should calculate how to retreat out of it without shame. But that he and his had been sarcastically and pitilessly handled in having such irons thrust into their souls he did not maintain long. It is usually so, except with the sternest of men. Human beings, in their generous endeavour to construct a hypothesis that shall not degrade a First Cause, have always hesitated to conceive a dominant power of lower moral quality than their own; and, even while they sit down and weep by the waters of Babylon, invent excuses for the oppression which prompts their tears.

This is a typically ironic comment from Hardy on the unmoral nature of the universe, and in the inability of any Deity to exercise benevolence or even justice to men. Yet this bitter irony refers to a tragedy which appears to be almost entirely the result of human weaknesses. Eustacia and Wildeve set out on their reckless flight, in which each of them abandoned a marital partner, out of a mixture of discontent, boredom, and resentment, and the resultant disaster must be blamed mainly on themselves. Any remaining blame surely attaches to Clym himself, who by his partly unjust anger and slowness to take steps to effect a reconciliation, has continued to alienate Eustacia. In view of the human causes of the tragedy, it seems totally unjust of the author to blame an unmoral First Cause, and wildly inappropriate to speak of 'the oppression which prompts their tears'. Hardy's overt comment here goes against the meaning of his own narrative.

In his dialogue, Hardy is best described as uneven. Those who allege that his dialogue represents nothing but decadent literary tradition can point to numerous examples, even in the best novels. The truth is that there are moments in his writing when Hardy's creativity flags somewhat, so that he falls back on the lifeless, faded literary speech of tradition. But again, there are numerous examples to be found in his work of simple, direct, and moving speech, especially in moments of crisis.

Nature

As is appropriate in a man who is noted for novels depicting a rural environment, one of Hardy's major strengths lies in his portrayal of nature. He is supremely conscious of the importance of the natural world, which he sees as the source of man's energies, his livelihood and, if properly used, his happiness. Man can only attain his full dignity and nobility if he lives in harmonious submission to the natural order, as characters like Gabriel Oak and Giles Winterborne do.

Hardy's observation of nature, as exemplified in his descriptive passages, is impressive, being accurate in detail, precise and expert, while not losing in detail a sense of the grandeur and unity of the whole natural universe. Such descriptions have the confident mastery of a writer who genuinely knows and understands the countryside. Consequently, one of the most noteworthy aspects of Hardy's works is the impressive visual pictures which he gives the reader. One can think of numerous examples from all the novels, but particularly memorable are the account of the great storm in *Far From the Madding Crowd,* the tree-planting scene in *The Woodlanders,* and the description of the lush pastures of Talbothays Dairy in *Tess.* Often, too, there is a powerful sense of a unity between the human being's emotions or moods and the natural scene: for example, the passage describing how Angel Clare feels every part of the dairy permeated by Tess's presence (*Tess,* Chapter XXV). Hardy is particularly good in his handling of the openings of his stories, which often commence with an unhurried description of the landscape, into which one or more human figures are then naturally and easily introduced to begin the action of the narrative.

Symbolism

Symbolism is one of Hardy's chief means of showing the unity of man with his natural and social environment. Sometimes, the images used to suggest this identity are too obvious and unsubtle: examples are little Father Time's comments on the flowers at the show in *Jude,* and Troy's display of sword play in *Far From the Madding Crowd.* But many symbols make Hardy's point powerfully and effectively: for example, Tess's incursion into the poisonous weeded garden, in which Angel Clare plays the harp; or Bathsheba's night spent, unknown to her, beside a poisoned swamp.

This use of symbolism emphasizes a most important feature of Hardy's art, which is that, even when writing in prose, he is primarily a poet, who, in his best work, achieves that harmony of style with subject-matter, and appropriate choice of words and images that we are accustomed to find in poetry. He is also primarily a poet who celebrates natural life, and therefore he succeeds best when he is depicting the natural world itself, and the great basic experiences of human beings: birth, love, marriage, death, the harvest, and work. Hardy's characters are noteworthy more for the basic emotions and experiences that they share with other human beings than for the exceptional skills and attributes that distinguish men and women from each other. He is less at ease in describing the world of cultivated society, and the kinds of attributes and manners that are the products of a highly civilized social order. Hardy's greatest strength is perhaps his belief in the natural worth and dignity of man; his greatest weakness is perhaps a somewhat cynical contempt for the achievements of civilization.

10

Hardy's Achievement

The final question which we must ask about Hardy is, how great was his achievement in prose writing? His standing in informed critical opinion is not as high today as it once was. He is little known internationally — it is significant that he never won the Nobel Prize for Literature — and he arouses limited enthusiasm among many modern English critics. Yet he remains a great popular novelist, whose books are still widely read and enjoyed in the English-speaking world.

From what has been said in earlier chapters on Hardy's defects as a writer, his limited appeal to many intellectuals can be readily understood. His is not a very profound or deeply logical mind. His ideas, which include evolutionary development, agnostic humanism, and the necessity for social improvement, now seem dated, frayed, and very unexciting. The illogicalities and inconsistencies of his thought are apparent in all his novels; the reader is frequently conscious of a degree of confusion in the author's mind about the unmoral universe and its First Cause, about fate, determinism and free will. Remediable social injustices are not clearly distinguished from the natural ills of the human condition, and there is a strange paradox in the low value that Hardy, a cultivated man himself, places on education and culture. His reasoning often seems laborious, and his characters' problems and misadventures, in themselves sometimes banal, are dealt with in a very weighty manner. And — a very serious defect to most modern critics — Hardy's prose style is often clumsy and laboured.

However, as well as glaring defects, Hardy possesses substantial virtues. His ideas about the world are neither profound nor very original, but his way of using these ideas is masterly. He expresses his ideas about life through the actions and feelings of characters who are vividly alive, with that seemingly independent life which is the result of genuine creative vitality. He possesses the simple, rare virtues of the born novelist: the skill to write a story that interests; and the ability to create characters in whose existence the reader believes.

Hardy's grasp of the world, and of the ideas which he obtained mainly from his reading, is primarily emotional and not intellectual, and, because of this, he expresses in his books an emotional and tragic view of the universe which is deeply compelling. Like all powerful writers, Hardy leads the reader to enter into the author's view of life. It is because of the force of his emotional beliefs that Hardy's books carry conviction to the reader.

Moreover, if Hardy's intellect is neither outstandingly original nor very subtle, his mind is nevertheless one of deep seriousness and integrity. He never took an opinion at second hand, nor, whatever the cost in suffering to himself, accepted any belief which seemed to him to be contrary to reason or experience. This kind of integrity has the disadvantage of cutting a writer off from traditional values and institutional attachments, which, if accepted, help him to integrate his views of the world; In *After Strange Gods,* T. S. Eliot, a devout Anglo-Catholic himself, criticized Hardy for the lack of submission to objective beliefs. Hardy, however, though he loses some qualities because of the intellectual isolation of his position, retains as a result of it the true artist's distinctive personal view of the universe, and his novels carry the stamp of this integrity.

Suffering and sadness are central to Hardy's work, in which the distresses and disappointments of humanity receive greater emphasis than happy experiences. To some, the stress which he lays on suffering may seem excessive, but in this tragic vision of the world, the product of a mind which broods upon the senseless injustice to be found everywhere, lies a profound truth which corresponds with the experience of every reader. Suffering and disappointment are the lot of every human being at some time; the most fortunate and fulfilled individual cannot escape natural sorrow, loss, and disappointment, even if he encounters nothing worse. Hardy makes suffering bearable by showing, through the fates of his unhappy characters, that it is universal, the common destiny, and can be mitigated by a recognition on the part of the individual that he is not unique, and by a consequent cheerful acceptance of the common burden of humanity. This perceptive vision of the essential imperfection of the world is of value, in particular, to the young reader, to whom, because he *does* expect the world to be perfect, every disappointment seems tragic, and every injustice outrageous. And Hardy exercises his great influence as a teacher because his counsel is not the facile advice of an uninvolved theorist, but the product of a mind genuinely sensitive to the sufferings of humanity, and infinitely tender and sympathetic to the unhappy and unfortunate.

Hardy also makes a profound popular appeal because he is the champion of natural goodness and worth. It has been noted that he undervalues the great civilized virtues and attainments that are developed by education and by social institutions; his denigration of these attributes tends to make him an uncongenial writer to the cultivated intellectual, who often attaches paramount importance to mental achievement and civilized values. But, in asserting that human goodness is more important than all talent, accomplishments, refinement, or beauty, Hardy is propounding a truth which commands a universal assent. Realistically, he does not depict goodness as necessarily receiving any reward in the world, nor did he believe in any compensatory rewards in a future life. Moral worth, which is what primarily distinguishes man from all other species, is simply valuable in itself. In Hardy's novels, the actions of the good, such as the sacrifice by Winterborne of his cot to Grace, or the honest confession of Tess to Clare — both of which are actions that lead to personal disaster for the agents — are seen to be intrinsically beautiful. The beauty of goodness is something which can be readily understood by every reader, and it accounts for much of Hardy's enduring popularity; it's artistic depiction is of particular value in the present age of shoddy values and cheap sensations.

Hardy primarily asserts the value of a goodness which might be termed innate, yet he also vividly depicts the struggles of men, usually poor and obscure, to attain moral worth. The most interesting struggles of his main characters are not those made for fulfilment or achievement (although these are sympathetically described in the cases of Jude, Henchard, and, to some extent, Clym), nor even the struggle for happiness (although most of Hardy's characters do try to attain this), but primarily the struggle to hold to goodness and truth and resist the darker and meaner temptations which assail the human soul. Hardy's greatest characters, which include Tess, Jude, Henchard, and Winterborne, all epitomize this struggle, which, because it is the fundamental struggle of human life, is of universal significance. T. S. Eliot, in *After Strange Gods*,[1] criticized Hardy for making his characters too easily subject to passion. He said:

> . . . those who abandon themselves without resistance to excitements which tend to deprive them of reason, become merely instruments of feeling and lose their humanity; and unless there is moral resistance and conflict there is no meaning.

Here Eliot, although an outstanding creative writer and a perceptive critic, was totally wide of the mark. It is precisely because there is struggle in Hardy's novels—weak or unavailing though that struggle may often be—that his books are deeply significant.

Hardy is also the great delineator in prose of rural England. He has a profound knowledge of the Wessex countryside, its distinctive way of life, and its pattern of culture, and this results in descriptions of outstanding accuracy. At his best, Hardy writes his descriptive prose with the feeling of a poet for the use of words, and for images and similes of startling aptness and freshness.

There is nobody to match Hardy in his portrayal of ordinary people. Their rich and pithy speech, their strange conversation consisting often of home-spun philosophy, and their self-deprecating manner are faithfully recorded. Some critics have termed him patronizing and facetious in his portrayal of the rustics, but this is to show the urban intellectual's lack of understanding of country people. The humour in Hardy's depiction of the work-people exemplifies his profound delight in their speech and idiosyncracies, and the rustics serve as genuine comic relief to the tragic vision of the major works.

The last word on Hardy may fitly be quoted from the work of the distinguished critic, Mrs Q. D. Leavis,[2] who, although she makes over-severe criticisms of his defects, nevertheless has a keen eye for his true qualities.

---

[1]T. S. Eliot, *After Strange Gods*, London, 1934.
[2]Q. D. Leavis, 'Thomas Hardy and Criticism', *Scrutiny* XI, 1943.

We can only be grateful for having a body of fiction that proceeds from so honest, worthy and compassionate a nature, so sensitive to human misery and so powerful to record its distresses at the spectacle of suffering, so disinterested unworldly and unfailingly tender.

Bibliography

Here is a brief list of suggestions for further reading.

Biography

Gittings, Robert, *Young Thomas Hardy*, London, 1975.
Hardy, Evelyn, *Thomas Hardy, A Critical Biography*, London, 1954.

Criticism

The following short works will be found useful: Cecil, David, *Hardy the Novelist*, London, 1943.

(Has many illuminating comments, but should not be regarded as a substitute for detailed study of the text of individual novels.)
Hawkins, Desmond, *Hardy the Novelist*, London, 1950 / Newton Abbot, 1965.

(Stimulating, but some of the analysis of character should be treated with caution.)
Johnson, Trevor, *Thomas Hardy*, London.
(Good short survey.)

A great number of full-length critical works on Hardy have been written. The four following are perhaps the most valuable.
Howe, Irving, *Thomas Hardy*, New York, 1967.
Millgate, Michael, *Thomas Hardy, His Career as a Novelist*, London, 1971.
Southerington, F. R., *Hardy's Vision of Man*, London, 1971.
Stewart, J. I. M., *Thomas Hardy*, London, 1971.
Further suggestions for reading will be found in these books.

Glossary

Below are given brief explanations of some of the literary expressions used in the text.

Image: an image is a word or phrase denoting a sensory experience, often visual. For example, we could speak of the boy Jude's *image* of the city of Christminster seen on the horizon. Metaphors and similes are often used to give vividness to this sensory experience, as for example in Shakespeare's sonnet beginning, "So are you to my thoughts as food to life . . ." An abstract idea personified may also be used as an image.

Symbol: a symbol is an object which stands for something else, which may often be abstract, besides its concrete meaning. For example, the cross is not only the object of wood or metal but the symbol of Christianity; an engagement ring is not only the precious object, but the indicator of the promise to marry between two people.

There are many examples of the use of symbols in Hardy's novels. Two noteworthy examples are contained in the scene in *Tess,* where Tess herself approaches Angel, who is playing the harp, through a poisonous garden. Here the harp symbolizes the appearance of outward goodness that Angel represents, while the noxious garden symbolizes the poison which he will introduce into Tess's life.

Realism: this term means writing which emphasizes truthfulness of detail in speech, description, etc., and shuns fantasy, flights of imagination, and the subjective approach. It deals with the commonplace events of everyday life, usually middle or lower-class life.

Pastoral: this means a conventional, stylized piece of literature, based on rural surroundings, and featuring familiar stock situations. One such situation is the love of a shepherd for his cruel mistress.

Determinism: this means the philosophical theory that all events, including moral choices, are completely determined by previous existing causes, and that therefore the individual is not free to exercise any real choice.

Free Will: this is the opposite philosophical theory to determinism. It means the ability of the individual to exercise choices, including moral choices, and the assumption that no law of causation, whether external constraint or inner compulsion, compels him to act in a specific way.

INDEX